COMEDY IMPROV- ✫ISATION

EXERCISES & TECHNIQUES FOR YOUNG ACTORS

by

Delton T. HORN

𝕞𝕡™

MERIWETHER PUBLISHING LTD.
Colorado Springs, Colorado

Meriwether Publishing Ltd., Publisher
Box 7710
Colorado Springs, CO 80933

Editor: Ted Zapel
Typesetting: Sharon Garlock
Cover design: Tom Myers

© Copyright MCMXCI Meriwether Publishing Ltd.
Printed in the United States of America
First Edition

Library of Congress Cataloging-in-Publication Data

Horn, Delton T.
    Comedy improvisation : exercises and techniques for young actors /
    by Delton T. Horn.
        p.   cm.
    ISBN 0-916260-69-0
    1. Improvisation (Acting)   2. Stand-up comedy.   I. Title.
PN2071.I5H67   1991
792.2'3'028--dc20
                                           90-28459
                                             CIP

PREFACE

There is no question that comedy is big today, and it's getting bigger. Almost every city of any size has at least one comedy club. Comedy showcases are frequently seen on TV, especially on cable. Let's face it, everyone enjoys a good laugh.

One of the most exciting forms of comedy is improvisational comedy, where the performers make up the script as they go along, often with active input from the audience. Perhaps part of the appeal of comedy improvisation is the element of risk involved. What if the performers can't think of anything to say or do? What if the improvised scene isn't funny?

Having worked with comedy improvisation for quite some time now, I've found that such disasters rarely, if ever, happen. Certainly some improvised scenes are far from classic moments in comedy, but they seldom die altogether. Audiences almost always are rooting for the improvisational performers to do well, and at the very least, the effort itself is entertaining.

A good comedy improvisation is like a party. Everyone (on stage and off) has a good time.

In my work with comedy improvisation, I have often been asked if I knew of a good book on the subject. I couldn't even find a bad one. So I decided to write one. A book on the subject, that is — not a bad one. (At least I hope not.)

In this book I will share my experience in forming and running a comedy improv group. Dozens of exercises and scene structures you can use are described fully.

Improvisation is a valuable skill for any comedian or other performer, even if you plan to use only fully scripted material. There is always a possibility of something going wrong, and improvisation can dig you out of the hole. Who knows? The results may be even better than the original script.

Many of the improv exercises are well suited to a classroom setting, and could be a very useful tool in training actors. Sometimes there is a tendency to look down on comedy, because it is so easy to get a cheap laugh. But a good comedy scene has everything a good dramatic scene has, *plus* the humor. I strongly believe that comedy is a great training ground for performers, even if their goal is to play only high tragedy.

Almost all of these improvisational exercises and structures are fun to do. Many of them would make great party games that even non-performers and habitual wall flowers can get into. When I've been involved with improv parties, I found that the people who are most shy to begin with often end up having the greatest fun of all. In a party situation, almost everybody can open up. With no audience, there is no excuse for stage fright. Everyone else there is "making a fool of himself or herself" too. It's good, clean fun.

Improvisation is also a useful tool for creating group-written scripts. The performers can try the scene out in a variety of ways, keeping what works, and rejecting what doesn't work.

And, of course, many of the scene structures described in this book are designed specifically for use in true performance situations on stage. Tips on dealing with audience and scheduling shows for maximum impact will also be discussed.

The comic improvisation structures presented in this book range from the very simple and basic, which almost anyone can do, to very sophisticated structures, which require considerable skill to pull off.

I sincerely hope you have as much fun with these comedy improvisation structures as I have had for the last several years. I intend to keep on having fun with them for years to come too.

Delton T. Horn

TABLE OF CONTENTS

CHARACTER IMPROV STRUCTURES

ADVANCED IMPROV STRUCTURES

ADVANCED ACTING EXERCISES

FORMING A COMEDY/IMPROV TROUPE

PUTTING ON AN IMPROV SHOW

PROTECTING YOURSELF AND YOUR WORK

Most theories of comedy focus on one or more of the following elements: surprise, recognition superiority, rebellion and aggression, and playfulness.

Chapter 1
THE BASICS OF IMPROVISATION AND COMEDY

This book is about comedy and improvisation, so it is probably reasonable to start out by defining our terms. This introductory chapter is largely theoretical, unlike most of the rest of this book. The theory may seem like a waste of time, but it is necessary to have some basis to build any practical work on.

Much of this material is rather subjective. There is no hard and fast "truth." Inevitably, I have had to rely heavily on my own opinions, based on my experiences and observations. Of course, you should feel free to disagree with me. What I have to say here is just a way to get you started in the area of comedy improvisation.

What Is Improvisation?

Just what is improvisation anyway? In the simplest possible terms, improvisation is a specialized form of acting in which no script is used. The actors make up all of their own dialog as they go along. In essence, the "script" is being written, directed, and performed simultaneously. The improvising actor takes over the job of the playwright. The actor also assumes the director's functions in staging the scene.

Improvisation can be used in many different ways, and for a variety of purposes.

Most acting classes today include at least some improvisational exercises. Improvisation is an excellent way for the actor to hone the various aspects of his craft. Specific improv exercises focus on specific acting problems. It is perhaps the ultimate in learning by doing. While this book's main focus is

1

on improvisational structures that can be performed before an audience, we will not ignore the classroom. Improv structures designed as acting exercises will be covered in Chapter 2.

Some directors have the cast of a play they are working on improvise scenes not actually in the script. This allows the actors to create characters with greater depth. To improvise a character well, you obviously must know the character very thoroughly, and the best way to get to know a character is to improvise dialog for him or her. The actor learns how to think "as the character."

A script for a play can even be created or polished through improvisation. The same scene is tried several times, each time keeping what works and rejecting what doesn't work. A number of theatrical works have been created in this way. Many experimental or avant-garde theatre groups have used this technique. Improvisation has also been an important factor in creating more "mainstream" plays, such as "Story Theatre," and the musical "You're a Good Man, Charlie Brown."

Some daring performance groups even improvise in front of a live audience. This is the type of improvisation that will be emphasized in this book. Personally, I got started with performance improvisation when I was too young and naive to realize it was supposed to be difficult. It is hard, but far from impossible to put on an entertaining show through improvisation. This tradition of improvising in performance dates back to the commedia dell'arte troupes of the Renaissance. Modern performance improvisation is exemplified by Second City. It is a very exciting art form. Much of its excitement grows from its inherently challenging nature.

In modern performance improvisation, the audience usually plays some part in the creation of the scene. This element of participation greatly heightens the theatrical experience. Generally, the performers take specific suggestions from audience members, then present a scene based upon those suggestions.

With very few exceptions, performance improvisation

tends towards comic scenes. Comedy and improvisation naturally go well together. The comic spirit thrives under the loose
"anything goes" atmosphere of improvisation, but the rules of
the improv structure prevent total chaos. Except for the more
basic acting exercises, improvisations usually work best when
they are comic in nature. Comedy improvisation is a lot of fun.

Many comedy improv structures make great party games
because they are so much fun to do. Enjoy them.

While some overly serious people might object to the idea,
comedy improvisation is also appropriate to the classroom if
it is controlled properly. Why shouldn't the learning experience
be fun? We actually learn best through controlled play. A touch
of humor tends to make the educational points "stick" better.
You can remember the heart of the lesson without trying so
hard to memorize it.

Improvisational acting exercises are also known as
theatre games. They work best when they are treated as games.
That is, they should be fun, or they lose much of their effectiveness. Allowing the improv exercises to be comic in tone is a
good way to make the learning experience enjoyable and effective. All of this will be covered in greater detail in Chapter 2.

Of course, the emphasis in this book will be on performing
comedy improvisations before an audience, but other types of
improvisation will also be covered because there is considerable
overlap between the various improvisational styles and applications.

The Commedia Dell'arte

It may be useful to take the time here for a brief glance at
history, covering the commedia dell'arte of the Renaissance
period. All modern improvisation, both in the classroom and on
the stage, owes a major debt to the commedia dell'arte performers.

Commedia dell'arte performers were professional actors,
traveling in troupes, and performing on makeshift stages. They
did not use any scripts, although a written scenario was em-
ployed. The scenario was just a rough plot outline, loosely de-

fining the essential action and the entrances and exits for each scene. The actors came up with their own dialog, which varied from performance to performance. Even when the same scenario was used, no two shows would be alike.

The story lines laid out in the scenario were usually pretty basic, relying on stock characters and comic situations whose origins can be traced back to the Greek "New Comedy" and the Roman comedies of Plautus and Terence, among others. Later these same stock characters and situations were further refined in the plays of Molière. They still turn up in modern situation comedies on television and in the movies.

For the most part, different commedia dell'arte companies used the same basic characters. Every troupe had its own Pantalone and Harlequin, for example. Most of the comic characters were played by actors wearing masks.

A commedia dell'arte performer specialized in a specific character, which he played throughout his career. Over the years, a performer would develop a number of stock bits that could be used in a variety of circumstances. These stock bits included memorized speeches (concetti), and stunts or pieces of comic business (lazzi).

You might object that this is not true improvisation, but nobody can improvise everything. A good improvisor must have a good memory for what has worked well in the past. If a piece of business which did well in a previous performance is appropriate to the current improv situation, there is no reason why it can't be reused with modifications as necessary.

There is a fine line that can be crossed here. If you are only doing bits that you have done before, then you aren't improvising. However, there is nothing wrong with mixing the old with the new. To a large extent, it is unavoidable. In any given scene, there are just so many possibilities. If you improvise a specific type of scene enough times, you are bound to repeat yourself in spots.

If elements of an improvised scene are repeated, that's OK. But if entire scenes are being repeated more or less verbatim, then you are not improvising. How much repetition should be allowed is a judgment call that must be made by each performance group. In the classroom, repetition should generally be discouraged. The point of most improvisation exercises is to try new things, not to polish old material.

Good commedia dell'arte performers were constantly creating new concetti and lazzi. They would try different things in each performance. The more experience the actor had, the larger his "bag of tricks" and the greater the possibilities that were open to him. A wealth of experience led to better improvisation in the commedia dell'arte. And the same thing is true today. The more you improvise, the better you will become at it. Knowing what has worked in the past does not limit improvisation. It simply gives the performer more control.

The Comic Spirit and Improvisation

Comedy and improvisation just naturally go well together. The comic spirit thrives on the spontaneous "anything goes" atmosphere of improvisation.

Many writers have speculated on what makes comedy "tick." Nobody can really explain why some things are funny and other things are not. I'm certainly not going to stick my neck out here and attempt to offer definitive answers. But I think it will be useful to consider some principles of comic theory as they apply to improvisation.

Comedy grows out of an ambiguous entity we can call the "comic spirit." This isn't metaphysics, just a convenient label for whatever quality makes something funny.

The comic spirit incorporates many things, including point of view and tone. Most theories of comedy focus on one or more of the following elements: surprise, recognition, superiority, rebellion and aggression, and playfulness.

We will briefly consider each of these elements as they apply to improvisation.

5

Surprise

Surprise is an important part of most jokes. How many jokes were funny the second time you heard them? You probably don't laugh the second time you hear a certain joke because you already know the punch line. There is no surprise.

Of course, surprise is inherently part of any improvisation. Because the actors are making up the "script" as they go along, nobody knows for sure what will happen next. Some degree of surprise is inevitable. Even the performers are likely to be surprised.

Surprise alone is not enough to create comedy. Just because something is unexpected, doesn't necessarily mean it's funny. The heaviest, grimmest tragedy will be full of surprises, or it will be boring.

The element of surprise is not essential for all types of comedy. Some things are even funnier when you know what is coming. I can watch old Laurel & Hardy shorts over and over again and still enjoy the comedy. I have practically memorized some of them from seeing them so often, so there is obviously no surprise involved anymore, but the films are still funny because of other comic elements.

Still, surprise is undeniably important in comedy overall. In improvisation, the inherent element of surprise lends itself well to the comic spirit. To some degree, the surprise element of improvisation is related to the element of playfulness, which will be discussed later.

Recognition

When we recognize a comic truth, we laugh. "Yes," we think, "that's the way it really is. Isn't it silly? Isn't it delightful?"

Humor based on recognition tends to be the most repeatable. It can be funny time after time. Often the element of surprise emphasizes the experience of comic recognition, so some recognition humor is at its funniest the first time you encounter it. But even when the element of surprise is lost, it is still amusing.

A good improvisation, whether comic or not, almost always demands the recognition element. If we cannot recognize (and understand) what is going on, the improvisational scene is not going to make any sense, naturally. On a more important but less obvious level, if we don't recognize the *truth* of what is happening, the scene won't have any point. It will just ramble on, and who cares?

Superiority

Most theorists on the subject of comedy mention the element of superiority. The foolishness of the comic characters presumedly make the audience feel better about itself. This, say the theorists, is why so many comic characters are presented as stupid, or possessing some other defect (cowardliness, greed, etc.) to a massive degree. On the other hand, if a comic character is not flawed, there isn't much room for humor. Perfection is not funny. If the character is not flawed, how can we laugh at him or her? There is nothing to make a joke about.

Personally, I believe the superiority element has been greatly over-stressed in theoretical writings on comedy. I think humor grows more out of the recognition of human foibles than any sense that we (the audience) are better than the comic characters. We recognize in comic characters our own flaws, or the flaws of people we know, and we laugh. The exaggeration of comedy makes this recognition less painful. We recognize our faults, but we're not as bad as the comic character. This is probably the extent of the superiority element in most comedy.

If the creator of a comic character feels too superior to that character, the character will almost surely fail. The character will not be believably motivated. The attempts at humor at the character's expense will tend to be heavy-handed, and unfunny. In performing, especially in an improvisational format, the actor must be very, very careful about the superiority element. Remember, the comic character is not funny to himself or herself. Nobody ever does things to show how stupid they are. The character must think he is behaving properly, or it won't work. This concept will be discussed in a little more detail in later sections on characterization.

Rebellion and Aggression

The comic spirit is naturally rebellious. It is the eternal enemy of all rules and regulations. It rejects serious traditions and cultural taboos. It twits sacred cows and pricks holes in dignity. It delights in anarchy and chaos. In a word, the comic spirit is "naughty." It has no interest in obeying anything beyond its own imperatives.

Too much rigidity in an improv structure will harm the chances for humor. It will also make the improvised scene tend to be dull and lifeless, even if you are doing a noncomic improvisation.

But you can go too far in the other extreme too. Too much anarchy will result only in a confused and decidedly unfunny muddle. The comic spirit works best within some kind of definite structure. The structure should be loose enough to permit the comic spirit to rebel, but it must also be tight enough to give the comic spirit something to rebel against. The tension between the natural anarchy of the comic spirit and the rules of the structure will heighten both.

Because of the rebellious nature of the comic spirit, comedy is often offensive. It gleefully breaks all taboos.

In recent years there has been a strong trend toward deliberate offensiveness and vulgarity in comedy. I even heard one comic state that the function of comedy is to offend. This is ridiculous. Actually, when you stop to think about it, comedy that offends can't amuse. Nobody ever laughs at anything that offends them. "Offensive" comedy works only when it is perceived as being offensive to someone else. The audience laughs to show its presumed superiority over the bluenoses who would be offended. Often people who might be mildly offended will laugh anyway, to show how hip and free they are. Some laughs may also be born of embarrassment, but they have little to do with true humor.

The true comic spirit will not go out of its way to be offensive. Nor will it go out of its way to avoid giving offense. It simply doesn't care if it's offensive or not.

In practical terms, any comic must consider the question of offensiveness. How far will you go in your material? In some performance situations you can get away with more than in others. In some comedy clubs, vulgarity and offensiveness seem to be expected. But this doesn't mean you have to go along with the expectations. You'll just have to work a little harder to keep it clean.

Every comic performer must set his or her own standards. As a general rule of thumb, I would advise steering clear of blatantly offensive or vulgar material, especially in an improvisational structure. For one thing, it seems a little foolish to risk losing a portion of your audience. Also, if you are in the habit of working clean, you will have no problem if you have to start performing in a more restrictive environment. Many comics have a real problem when they get a chance to do TV.

The most important reason to limit vulgar humor in improvs is that it is too easy. Often the only "joke" is "Ha, ha, ha! Somebody said something naughty!" It doesn't require much talent to get a cheap laugh out of a four-letter word. Good improvisation should be a constant challenge. If you go for the easy laughs, you'll rarely fail, but your successes won't be much more than mediocre. It will be hard to take any pride in your improv work if you aren't doing anything more than any moron could do just as well.

Vulgarity

I would never advocate any kind of censorship. Some vulgar or offensive humor is very, very funny when there is some wit involved. But when the offensiveness or vulgarity itself is all that's "funny," there doesn't seem to be much point to it. Comics who rely heavily on that type of cheap laugh are invariably either too untalented or too lazy to come up with anything better. While some enjoy some limited success, their abilities as performers peak early and then stagnate. Challenge yourself to constant new growth. Improvisation won't let you stagnate unless you cheat and take the easy route of cheapness.

Of course, four-letter words and vulgarity are only one type of offensiveness. Ethnic humor and stereotypes are also risky. Strongly political material or jokes about religion or moral issues will almost certainly lose some of your audience. I'm not saying you can't do such material. It could be argued that such material will create a stronger bond with those in the audience who agree with you. But you should always be aware of the price of offensiveness. It will always, by definition, limit your audience appeal.

On the other side of the coin, don't bend over backwards to try to avoid anything that could possibly give any offense to anyone. For one thing, it can't be done. The most innocuous and seemingly inoffensive joke will probably offend somebody. You can't worry about nuts who seemingly want to find something to be offended by. I am frequently surprised by the things some people complain about.

But if you know ahead of time that a joke is obviously a potential offender, you should consider whether it is worth doing. This is an individual subjective judgment call that must be made on a case-by-case basis.

Hostility

Comedy is often considered to be an act of aggression. Many theorists place considerable emphasis on hostility as a primary element of comedy.

Much comedy is unquestionably hostile. You just have to consider the style used by comedians such as Don Rickles, among others. But can the gentle childhood reminiscences of Bill Cosby be called aggressive or hostile? It might be more appropriate to consider comedy an act of criticism rather than aggression. Virtually all humor implies that something is wrong. If something was perfect, how could anyone make a joke about it? Perfection isn't funny. Some criticism is aggressive and hostile and some is not. I think this is true of comedy too.

Generally, real aggressive, hostile humor doesn't work too

well in improvisation. It tends to be threatening to the audience, making people less likely to laugh. It also makes them more likely to heckle. If the performer is hostile, the audience will be too. This type of problem will be discussed in a later chapter.

Playfulness

Probably the most important element in humor is fun, or playfulness. If it isn't fun, it's not going to be funny. The audience, of course, must find the experience enjoyable, but the performers should be having a good time too. The performers must not appear to be working at being funny, or the delicate air of comedy will be lost. It is hard work, but the effort must never show.

Much of the assumed hostility and superiority elements of comedy are really, in my opinion, just playfulness. Watch some puppies at play some time. They growl and bare their teeth at each other, then they jump one another and wrestle. But there is no real aggression in them. They are just playing.

Much of the apparent aggression of comedy is due to the dramatic need for conflict (discussed shortly). Without conflict there is no action or story. Conflict implies two or more forces at odds with one another, so the appearance of aggression is somewhat inevitable.

The Elements of Successful Improvisation

A good improvisation is a form of drama. The fact that the scene is being "written" as it is performed doesn't alter the requirements of drama. There are certain elements which are essential for any successful scene, including improvisational scenes.

There are four basic elements that the improvisor should keep in mind at all times. They are: characters, setting, conflict and action, and dialog and humor. Each of these elements will be discussed in the next few pages.

Characters

Specific people must be involved in the scene. Too many newcomers to improvisation neglect characterization. They may come up with a string of witty, clever lines, but the scene as

11

a whole will never take off with any life of its own.

The characters don't necessarily have to be human. In more fanciful improvisations, the characters could be dogs, hamsters, trees, or almost anything else the imagination may come up with. While the characters don't have to be human, they must be recognizable as "people." That is, they must have human characteristics and motivations.

The audience must know just who the characters are, or the scene will almost certainly be boring. If we don't care about the people involved, how can we care about what happens to them?

All characters must be motivated. Unfortunately, the term "motivation" has gotten a bad rap in many circles due to the extremism of too many method actors. There are many bad "method actors." For example, an actor is told to play a man who has been alone on a deserted island for years and now he is joined by a beautiful woman, and the actor asks "What's my motivation?" This is a slight exaggeration, but it is typical of many "method actors." Of course, these actors don't really understand motivation at all.

Motivation just means that nobody ever does anything without a reason. Some motivation is very superficial. Someone might scratch for no reason beyond the fact that he has an itch. On the other hand, many motivations are deep set and subtle, and sometimes even unconscious.

Interesting characters will have interesting motivations. If the characters are not trying to accomplish something (no motivation), your improvisation will end up as a very static, uninteresting scene.

The issue of motivation is also involved in the element of conflict and action, which is discussed later.

Setting

Any scene has to take place somewhere. It shouldn't be set in a vacuum, even though many improvisations are played that way.

The location will generally influence the course of the scene, at least to some degree. As an example, consider a scene in which a couple has an argument. Won't they behave differently if they are alone in their bedroom than if they are in a crowded restaurant? A more subtle, but still real difference would result if the scene was moved from the couple's bedroom to their kitchen.

While actual props are not normally used in improvisations, good improvisational performers will interact with objects in their environment or setting. These objects may be just referred to, or they may be mimed. Specific objects add to the realism of the setting, and therefore the effectiveness of the scene. Specific details are always more effective dramatically than generalities.

Conflict and Action

Something must be happening, of course, or there is no scene. People standing around agreeing with each other is almost always boring. Characters in conflict are the driving force in any scene, improvised or written.

Conflict is based on motivation. The characters want something. If what one of them wants is in opposition to what the other one wants, they will be in conflict.

All conflicts do not have to be heavy, screaming arguments. Subtle conflicts can also be very effective in drama. Here are some simple scene ideas with strong inherent conflicts:

— A door-to-door salesman and a reluctant customer;

— A nervous worker asking his boss for a raise;

— A couple of young lovers, each wanting the other to be the first to say "I love you";

— Two friends discussing their different feelings about a mutual acquaintance.

All of these scenes have built-in conflicts which will make them easier to play.

13

Dialog and Humor

In most improvisations, especially by beginners, considerable emphasis is placed on what is being said. That is, the dialog. In comedy improvisation there is a strong tendency to go for the jokes. The dialog is crammed full of snappy (hopefully) punch lines.

Actually, this should be treated as the least important element in a good improvisational scene. If you have well defined characters in a specific setting acting out a strong conflict, the dialog will tend to take care of itself.

There is usually a tendency to use too much dialog in improvs. The characters talk. If the characters are well defined and have a good conflict between them, dialog can certainly carry a lot of interest. But generally, the scene will be even more effective if it contains action. Instead of just talking, the characters should do something. Once again, interacting with the setting and mimed props will be a big help.

Some of the workshop exercises in Chapter 2 don't permit any dialog at all, forcing the actors to use action instead.

Since we are primarily concerned with comedy improvisation in this book, we naturally want our improv scenes to be funny. Performers often strain for punch lines, neglecting the other dramatic elements. When this happens the scene is only as good as the last joke. If a punch line fails, the scene fails.

Performers who try to come up with punch lines are the most likely to freeze up. If they can't think up a good joke on the spot, they may have trouble keeping the scene going. Even if the actors don't freeze up, this emphasis on punch lines almost invariably hurts their performance. Nobody can think up a good punch line each and every time. If you have nothing going for you beyond the punch lines, a few jokes that bomb are going to hurt.

Generally, it is best not to try to force the laughs. Ideally, the humor should grow naturally out of the other three elements. The richest comedy tends to occur when the characters don't appear to be aware that they are being funny. Characters who constantly reel off one liners aren't very interesting, at least not for long. Once again, the problem goes back to motivation. If the primary motivation is to tell jokes, there won't be a strong conflict and the scene will lose dramatic interest.

Of course, if in the course of an improv you happen to think of a really good punch line that is appropriate to the character and the scene, you should certainly use it. Just don't concentrate on thinking up punch lines. Focus on the dramatic principles of the scene.

It may sound contradictory, but often the best comedy improvs result when the actors aren't really trying to be funny. If you've got good comic characters in a good humorous situation, the laughs will come almost by themselves.

A Few General Rules

An improvised scene must follow definite rules to keep it from being pure chaos. This is true of any type of improvisation, whether in a classroom or workshop, or on stage before an audience. Most of the rules will vary with the specific improv structure. The following chapters will describe a number of improv structures for you to use. Essentially, each structure is a specific set of rules for performing the improv.

There are some general rules that should be followed regardless of the individual structure. These rules apply to all structures.

In some cases certain rules must be decided upon for each improv group. There is no definitive "right" answer, but all of the performers must be following the same rules. For example, earlier in this chapter I mentioned that the use of four-letter words is a decision that must be made by each group. If one actor is playing clean, and a second continuously uses profanity, they probably will not work too well together. They are not following the same rules.

In this section I will outline a few general rules which I believe should be adopted by all improv groups. Of course, you always have the freedom to disagree with me on any issue. A book like this can only advise. But I must warn you, I have

15

never seen a successful improvisation that did not follow these rules. They are not arbitrary.

1. *Know the structure thoroughly.* If the performers don't know the rules of the structure, how can they possibly do it well? Rehearse the structure until it is almost second nature. If you have to consciously think about the rules you will be distracted from your improvising. Each structure should be discussed thoroughly among the group, so that everyone knows the rules. Everyone must follow the same rules for the scene to work.

2. *Don't showboat.* Good improvisation is a team effort. The actors should not try to upstage one another. They should work together, not against each other. Always remember that if one performer looks bad, all of the performers in the scene will look bad.

3. *Know your partners.* Because good improvisation is a team effort, the best scenes will result from actors who can almost "read each other's mind." They sense when their partner is leading somewhere and they go along. Or they sense when the other is stuck and help out. They work together. A good improvisation team should know one another very well. Don't skimp on rehearsal. The more scenes you improvise together, the better your performance together will be.

4. *Listen to other people on stage.* This is probably one of the most important rules, and it is one of the most frequently broken. Characters in a scene must interact. Don't do a monolog. Don't pre-write the scene. Let it develop, with all of the performers contributing. Once again, it must be a team effort. Remember, no matter how good you are, someone else may have a better idea. If you don't listen to their dialog, you might miss out. And your dialog probably won't be very good either if it is not appropriate to the scene.

5. *Don't let a scene run too long.* The best improvs are probably fairly short. If a scene isn't going well, don't prolong the agony. If the scene is going well, get out while you're ahead. Don't let it run down. Work toward a resolution or strong ending

of the scene. Don't go past the natural ending. As you gain more experience, you will get better at recognizing a strong ending line when it comes up. If you are performing where you have control over the lights (some improvisation performances are not on true stages), blackouts can give a clear, smooth ending to an improv scene. The lighting operator should be considered a full member of the improv group and should attend the rehearsals. You will be relying on his judgment to determine when the scene should end.

6. *Explain the structure to the audience.* The audience needs to know what is going on or it won't understand or enjoy the improvisation. An emcee (who should be a member of the performing group) should preface the improv with a brief explanation of how the scene will work. Don't over explain. Keep it concise and to the point. The explanation should be combined with taking the necessary suggestions from the audience.

7. *Speak up.* If the audience can't hear what you're saying, the improv won't work, no matter how brilliant and creative you are. Learn to project. With very few exceptions, my advice to most actors would be if you think you are talking too loud on stage, try talking a little louder. Don't shout. The trick is to learn to project. Breathe from the diaphragm and speak clearly. Concentrate on making your voice carry to all parts of the audience.

8. *Have fun and don't worry.* Improvisations are basically games. They should be enjoyed by the performers as well as the audience. If the actors are miserable and straining to get through the scene, the unpleasant feeling will inevitably spread out to the audience. Naturally you want to do the best improvs you can, but don't get too hung up over it. By definition, improvisation involves taking chances. Inevitably, some of your improvs are going to flop. The risk makes successful improvs that much more exciting. Try to consider the challenge part of the fun of improvisation.

9. *Don't deny.* Once a statement has been made in an improv, it is part of the reality of the scene. Don't contradict

17

what your partner says. If, for example, one performer says, "Why are you wearing that stupid looking hat?", the other actor should *not* say, "I'm not wearing a hat." Sure, it's often an easy way to get a laugh, but it breaks the reality of the scene. It's the kind of laugh that can only harm the improvisation as a whole.

If your partner introduces an element you're not crazy about, you're stuck with it. But there is nothing that says you can't change the subject. Instead of saying "No," get in the habit of saying, "Yes, and —."

If you follow these simple, almost common-sense rules and the rules of the individual structure you are working on, you should not have any problem performing any improvisation, whether on stage, in the classroom, or in a workshop.

"Mirror, Mirror" is a very useful exercise. It should be performed frequently.

Chapter 2
IMPROVISATION IN
THE CLASSROOM

Most people find the whole idea of improvisation very intimidating. After all, it's very difficult, isn't it? Well, in a way. But it's been my experience that almost anybody can learn how to do it if they can get past the intimidation of the task. The first step in teaching improvisation is to soothe these common but unnecessary fears.

When teaching improvisation I usually start out by asking each student a question. The exact question doesn't really matter, as long as it doesn't call for a purely factual answer. In other words, don't ask "What is two plus two?" Instead, use questions like, "If you had a million dollars, what would you buy first?" or "What do you see yourself doing ten years from now?" or "Who is your favorite comedian?"

After everyone has answered a question, I point out that no one should have any trouble learning how to improvise. After all, they've just done it. They were not reading from scripts. They didn't know what I was going to ask, so they couldn't preplan their answers. They had to improvise.

We all improvise every single day of our lives. Every conversation we have is a little improvised scene. We write the "script" as we go along.

The main difference between stage improvisation and life improvisation is that on stage, improvisations usually have very definite and clearly defined rules that aren't there for most life improvisations.

What Improvisation Is Not

Many acting classes teach something they call improvisation, but it isn't. While some acting students find these exercises stimulating, most just feel rather foolish.

While adherents of certain schools of acting would disagree, I've never found much point to improvisations in which the actor portrays a tree or an ice-cream cone. There are very, very few parts for trees and ice-cream cones in plays. Even if there were such parts, they would unquestionably be highly personified. What would be important would be the human-like elements of the character. The superficial details, like how a tree stands, or how fast an ice-cream cone melts, can easily be researched when and if the need ever arises. If there is a solid basis of characterization to build on, an actor can play any animal or object just by tacking on the appropriate surface details.

These so-called "improvisations" do nothing to strengthen the student's characterization skills. I have seen no particular correlation between the ability to do well in such "improvisations" and the ability to perform well on stage.

The classroom improvisations presented in this chapter all pragmatically focus on specific essential stage skills. They aren't empty exercises for their own sake.

Some of the improv exercises described here work best if the actor does not know the point ahead of time. An example is the simple question exercise described at the beginning of this chapter. If the students know what I'm leading up to, the exercise will not be as effective. When I do conduct an improvisation exercise with a hidden point, my students always know that I'll explain my reasons when the time is right.

In the exercise descriptions to follow, I will point out what (if anything) should be concealed from the actor ahead of time, as well as what the teacher or director should be looking for during the improvisation.

Considerable emphasis is placed on making the exercises as enjoyable and entertaining as possible. It is exceedingly difficult to make an improvisation work effectively, even in the classroom, if the actors are bored. As you move on to the performance improvisation structures in later chapters of this book, you will see how many of them are merely extensions of the classroom improv exercises presented here.

Group Activity

"Group Activity" is an excellent exercise to use in early classes, or when forming a new improvisational group. It is a simple, nonthreatening exercise that strengthens cooperation and emphasizes paying attention to the other performers. Even in established groups, it would be worthwhile to repeat this exercise occasionally to reaffirm the necessary interaction.

One reason this exercise is so nonthreatening is because everyone is involved in the improvisation itself. Nobody has to be concerned about the possible reactions of a critical audience because there should be no audience. Even the teacher or director may participate in the "Group Activity" exercise.

The rules for this structure are very simple. No dialog or props are allowed. One person in the group is selected to begin. He gets on stage and starts to pantomime some simple activity. As other members of the group realize what the activity is, they also get on stage and join in the activity. They may duplicate the specific activity of the first performer, or (preferably) they may engage in a related activity.

For example, if the general activity is "gardening," the first performer may start out by pulling imaginary weeds. A second performer might start raking up these pulled weeds. A third might start planting seeds, and a fourth performer might water the garden. Cooperative activities are encouraged. For instance, the performer watering the garden may be joined by another performer to help guide the hose or to turn the water on and off.

For best results, encourage the starting performer to choose a simple, obvious activity with a number of possible variations. I've already mentioned gardening. Other possible "Group Activity" choices might be painting a house, or loading a moving truck. One of the most inventive "Group Activity" exercises I've seen started out with one person conducting. The other performers in the group started playing the various imaginary instruments in a mimed orchestra. Nobody tried to imitate the sounds of their instruments (which would be inappropriate to the exercise). The orchestra played silently and most of the performers even paid close attention to the conductor's gestures, playing only when he indicated they should. I was quite impressed by the cooperation shown by the group in this exercise.

Of course, for most group activities, there won't be a definite leader-figure like the conductor in the orchestra. In some activities, small groups of two or three people may focus in on one specific aspect of the general activity. Some of the performers may work alone, but they should not isolate themselves. Everyone in the group should be aware of what the others are doing. If two or more performers get in the way of each other's activities, they aren't paying close enough attention to the group nature of the exercise. Of course, these performers should not be harshly criticized and told they are doing it wrong. They should be encouraged to cooperate more directly the next time through the exercise. If someone seems to be having trouble with this exercise, advise them to help another performer with his or her task the next time around, rather than work alone.

It is very important that no talking (or sound effects) be permitted once the exercise has begun. The activity being performed should not be named out loud. The performers must be paying attention to figure out what they should do. If somebody makes a mistake and starts miming the wrong activity, they should not be criticized. Hopefully, they will quickly realize their mistake and start miming a more appropriate action.

The only talking permitted during the course of the exercise is limited to the teacher or director, and he should say as little as possible. About the only thing he should say during the exercise is to softly encourage any reluctant performers to get up on stage and join in. "Go ahead, John. Why don't you get involved now?" Of course the teacher or director also needs to talk when it is time to call a halt to the exercise. "OK. Good. That's enough."

After the exercise, let the group discuss it briefly. Were we

24

cooperating, or working individually? Was everyone involved with the same activity? If not, what caused the confusion? Do *not* assign blame for any such problems. Concentrate on how they could have been prevented by more awareness and cooperation by the group *as a whole.*

No one should "showboat" or draw attention to themselves as individuals in this exercise. Remember, this exercise is called "Group Activity." The important thing is to function as a group.

For best results, try the exercise two or three times with different activities. Of course, you should change the starting performer each time.

Group Story

This is another nonthreatening exercise that involves the group. The performers do not have to get on stage for this one. It works best if everyone is seated in a circle.

The group, as a whole, is to tell a story. Each person speaks just one word at a time in sequence. As long as the sentences are more or less correct grammatically, the exercise is going well. Don't expect the "story" to make any sense.

Avoid getting caught in a rut of endlessly repeating lengthy phrases. This is not a memorization exercise.

To do well in "Group Story," everyone in the group must listen to what is being said by the others. Do *not* try to preplan something clever to say. One of the performers ahead of you will inevitably say something to derail your plans, possibly leaving you stumped. Keep your mind clear and free-associate. Say the first grammatically appropriate word that comes to mind.

An important factor of this exercise is to keep it moving. The performers should not hesitate while they try to think of what to say. They should be encouraged to go with their very first impulse. As the group gets used to this exercise, you might want to see how fast they can keep the story moving.

If the story gets hopelessly bogged down (and it frequently

will, especially with beginning groups), the director or teacher should simply stop the story in midstream and instruct the group to start over with a completely new story.

The director or teacher should make the group aware that the story itself is not really important. This is an exercise, not a performance. The important thing is the cooperation and concentration involved in keeping the group story going.

Mirror, Mirror

The mirror exercise, in one form or another, is part of almost every acting class I have encountered. It is a very useful exercise, and should be performed frequently.

One curious thing that I've noted over the years is that actors and students either love this exercise, or they hate it. Few people are neutral on this one. Even those who hate it should grit their teeth and try it now and again anyway. Some actors and students who initially hate it eventually learn to love it. Others continue to hate it, but they *can* learn from the exercise.

These highly polarized reactions are not particularly surprising when you consider the nature of the exercise. It absolutely demands full cooperation with your partner. You cannot showboat or be the "star." The mirror exercise also concentrates the actors' attention so that any tendency toward self-consciousness is exaggerated. This can be a very uncomfortable feeling for many people.

When they give it a chance, most actors and students find the mirror exercise is both easier and harder than they expected.

"Mirror, Mirror" is performed in pairs. One performer is the Leader, and the other is the Reflection. The Reflection must duplicate any and all actions performed by the Leader. No speaking is permitted in this exercise.

That's all there is to the exercise, at least in concept. To do it well demands full concentration and cooperation between the two performers. They must learn to communicate nonverbally.

As performers get better at this exercise, they will increasingly tend to look into one another's eyes, rather than directly watching the bodily movements of the other.

Each pair of performers should perform this exercise twice during any session where the exercise is used. Each should have a turn as Leader and a turn as Reflection.

In a general acting class, various pairings should be made. Everyone should have the opportunity to perform the exercise with several different partners. If self-consciousness is a problem, you can start out by pairing off the entire class and have everyone perform the exercise the first couple of times simultaneously. The removal of any audience may ease some of the tension that sometimes can surround beginners in the mirror exercise.

In a performance troupe, every possible pairing should go through this exercise occasionally. Any two performers who will ever appear on stage together (especially in any kind of improv situation) should know how to cooperate with one another as much as possible. This requires them to know and anticipate each other. "Mirror, Mirror" is an excellent exercise for building up the necessary rapport between performers. Of course, any standardized teaming of performers could be strengthened with extra sessions of the mirror exercise.

The performers, especially those unfamiliar with the exercise, should be encouraged to use relatively slow, smooth movements. The Leader should *not* attempt to trick or confuse his Reflection. This is a cooperative, not a competitive, exercise.

As a pair of performers gets better at the mirror exercise and learns to anticipate one another accurately, they may try to get a little fancy. A well-choreographed "Mirror, Mirror" sequence can even be suitable as a performance piece. Such mirror routines were popular in vaudeville comedy. A classic and well-executed mirror routine is featured in the Marx Brothers' film, "Duck Soup."

Sense Memory

Many schools of acting talk a lot about sense memory. The term is often used to mean a number of things. For our purposes here sense memory is the ability to recall and simulate specific physical sensations and attributes without the normal stimulus. In improvisation, actors must frequently mime various props. Even in a scripted play, fake props that only approximate the real thing are often used. In order to make mimed or simulated props seem real to the audience, they must first become "real" to the actor.

The workshop leader, teacher or director should provide a number of common and uncommon objects. Only one is used at a time.

Everyone in the workshop should sit in a large circle. An object is handed to one of the actors. The actor should get to know the object. Feel its shape. How heavy is it? Does it have any particular smell? Does it make a sound? Is it brightly colored, or rather drab? What is special or unusual about this particular object? The actor should think about these questions, but not attempt to answer them out loud. Encourage the actor not to form verbal descriptions in his mind. Instead, he should try to memorize the physical sensations he gets from the object.

After a minute or two, the first actor passes the object on to the next actor, who goes through the same process. The object is passed completely around the circle.

When all of the actors have familiarized themselves with the object, it is put away. Then the object goes around the circle again, but this time it is mimed. Each of the actors should try to recreate within himself the physical sensations of the object.

Like everything else, sense memory gets better with practice. On the first try almost no one does very well, and most people feel rather foolish trying to mime the object in detail. Don't let anybody quit or make a joke of the exercise. They will get better with a little practice. We just aren't used to using our brains in this fashion.

There are many possible variations on this sense memory

exercise. Perhaps the actors could explore an object while blindfolded. Can they identify unfamiliar objects? Can they distinguish between similar but nonidentical objects? The absence of sight forces the mind to focus on the other senses.

Another variation is for each actor to familiarize himself with an object unseen by the others. He must then mime handling the object for the group. Can they describe the unseen object from how the actor interacts with it?

A shorter version of the basic sense memory exercise is called "Passing the Ball." Again, the entire group sits in a circle. They pass an invisible (mimed) ball around the circle. Nobody hangs onto the ball for more than a second or two. As the ball moves around the circle, the director or teacher should call out changes in the physical characteristics of the ball. For example: "It's getting larger"; "It's much lighter now"; "The surface is no longer slick, but rough"; "The ball is getting heavier"; "It's smaller now"; and so forth. The actors must immediately react to each of these changes. You should be able to "see" the ball change by how the actors handle it.

Defining Location

Actors should be able to define a location by sense memory. In this exercise, each actor should choose some specific location he is very familiar with. You might want to tell the actors to familiarize themselves with an appropriate location at the end of one rehearsal or class session, and perform the actual exercise the next time the group meets.

The actor should not tell anyone what his location is. He should get on stage and use sense memory to place himself in the location. He is not permitted to speak. He can interact with mimed objects. His general manner should be appropriate to the location. (Most people will stand and move somewhat differently in a football stadium than in a church, to use a rather extreme example.) The actor should also react to any physical stimuli of the environment itself. Is it hot or cold? Is it noisy? Is it crowded or empty? Is it spacious or cramped?

The other students or actors must identify the type of location the actor is portraying. They don't have to specifically identify a location they are not familiar with, of course. If they know they are in a doctor's office, for instance, they don't need to know which doctor owns the office.

If students seem to be having trouble with this exercise, tell them to consider the following questions: "Is it hot or cold here?" "Is this location spacious or cramped?" "What kind of activity might be performed here?" "Are there any other (imaginary) people here?" "What mood does this location create?" "Do you like it here, or do you want to leave?"

This exercise is surprisingly difficult to do well. It should be tried several times at different sessions. Once again, almost everyone will get better with practice.

Incidentally, when first describing the exercise to your group, advise them that it is cheating to use the stage or rehearsal area as their location. If you don't specifically forbid this choice, some wise guy will almost certainly come up with this "clever" idea. He'll get a laugh, but he won't get the benefit of doing the exercise properly.

Character Identification

Characterization is vastly important in all forms of acting. Even though characterization is often ignored by some improvisational performance groups, it is possibly even more important for good improvisation.

Characterization is not just saying "My name is George, and I'm a twenty-seven-year-old milkman." Real people are more than just a collection of superficial details like name, age and occupation.

A good characterization exercise is for each student or actor in the group to study some person known to the individual performer, but preferably *not* known to the group as a whole. In the actual improvisation, the actor plays the character of this person. The rest of the group then discusses what this person is like. If the actor did his job well, they will be very accurate on most things. If the group makes too many wrong assumptions about the character, the actor obviously has not done a sufficient characterization.

It is best if the group does not know the person being portrayed. A single distinctive trait (such as a characteristic stance or gesture) could identify the person, and the performer will not have to work at revealing any other aspects of the characterization because the other group members can fill in the blanks on their own from knowing the real person.

Of course, if the actor uses a person that the rest of the group doesn't know, the exercise must rely on the honor system. Only the individual student himself can really know how well or how poorly he did. It is very easy to cheat. No matter what the group says about the character, the dishonest student can claim that they are exactly right, no matter what the real person is like. In using this exercise in a workshop, emphasize to your actors that such cheating will only get in the way of them benefitting from the exercise.

The actual improvisation may take any of several forms. Personally, I lean toward using a nonspeaking scene. This will prevent the actor from giving too obvious verbal clues.

The character may interact with an object, or try to accomplish some physical task. An alternate approach which might be even more useful, is to place two or three (no more) actors on the stage at once, each playing their own specific characters. The situation should be simple. They could be waiting for a bus, or standing in line, or grocery shopping. Encourage the actors to react to one another's characters. Is that other character attractive to your character? Is he intimidating? Is he repulsive? How does one character affect another?

If some actors seem to be having a problem with this exercise, encourage them to use an "internal monolog." That is, they should think of the specific words of a speech by the character (about the situation and the other character or characters in the scene). The internal monolog should not be spoken aloud, but the actor should use the same level of concentration as if he were actually speaking out loud. Tell the actors, "Don't generalize feelings. Form specific words and sentences in your mind."

In some cases, it may be necessary to use some low-key dialog in a multicharacter scene. As much as possible, the dialog should be limited to the specific situation. The characters should *not* directly identify or describe themselves through dialog.

Randomly Selected Characters

In the last exercise, the actors got to choose their own characters. In most performance situations, the actor does not have this luxury. In a play, the character is defined by the script. In an improvisation, the specific structure and audience suggestions or the situation will require certain elements in the characterization. The actor is still free to add more elements and depth to the basic minimum characterization required. In fact, for a good performance, the actor *must* develop the character beyond the necessary givens.

In this exercise, the actors are given certain randomly selected elements of characterization and must build a character and perform a scene accordingly.

I generally use a number of prepared index cards to randomly select the character. The cards are divided into two decks. One deck (deck A) has a noun describing a character on each card. I've found that it is usually best to use professions such as cop, astronaut, teacher, cowboy. Some of the cards may not be true professions, but more or less social roles, such as hobo, mother, student. For our purposes here, such social roles can be considered as professions.

The second deck of index cards (deck B) features adjectives describing the character's state of mind. Some examples include angry, paranoid, lonely, overly helpful, confused. For whatever reason, most actors find it easier to play more negative emotions — sadness and anger are easier than happiness. Keep this in mind while making up the cards for this exercise.

Each actor draws two cards — one from deck A and one from deck B. These two cards define in a very rough, minimal way, the character the actor must portray. For example, angry cop, lonely teacher, nosy dancer.

Because of the inherent randomness of the character selection process, some combinations may be very difficult to portray. For this reason, I usually allow each actor to reject one (and only one) card and draw a replacement. Do not, however, permit the actors to go through the deck until they find a combination they like. The temptation to pick an easy combination is too great to resist, and the actors will not get the full benefit of being challenged by the exercise.

The actors are put on stage two at a time. (Once the group has gotten to an advanced state, you might want to experiment with three or four character scenes, but this tends to be very difficult. For a less experienced group, stick with two character scenes. Among other benefits, this forces everybody to participate fully in their scenes. Nobody can sit back and let somebody else do all the work.) The two actors must play a scene between their randomly selected characters. Depending on the make-up of your individual group, this improvised scene may be free form, or you may offer a structure to be followed. If possible, keep it as free form as possible. Force the actors to concentrate on characterization, rather than plot.

As in all improvisational exercises, emphasize that the actors should not try to be clever and witty. They should be true to their characters, not pasting on superficial jokes.

If the actors have difficulty making the scene move, advise them to think of something they are trying to accomplish in the scene. In other words, they should form a motivation that suits the character.

Sometimes it helps to use a third deck (deck C) of index cards. Each pair of actors randomly draws one card from deck C. The cards in deck C are marked with general locations, such as a church, a grocery store, a classroom, an airport. Often, placing the characters into a location will help the actors get the scene going.

Whether you use deck C or not, always remember that no scene should ever take place in a vacuum. If a location is not assigned, the actors should create one as part of the improvisation.

Nonverbal Communication

Just about everyone has heard about body language. We all use it every day. I'm sure everyone reading this has at some point sensed when a friend or loved one was troubled even though no words had been spoken. Often when someone says something, you can tell that they're lying. Their body language doesn't fit with their words. Without really thinking much about it, most people understand that nonverbal communication is more important than verbal communication in determining how someone else is really feeling. What is said is secondary to how it is said.

This is all pretty basic and obvious. But a surprisingly large number of people forget all about nonverbal communication when they get on stage. They're only concerned with what they're saying — the words.

To counteract this tendency, it is useful to practice some exercises in which words are forbidden. The actors must communicate by other nonverbal means.

There are several approaches you can take to nonverbal communication exercises. Some of the earlier exercises presented in this chapter were nonverbal, but we are considering more advanced nonverbal communication here. I will outline just a few nonverbal communication improv structures here.

In prehistoric times, early people were surely communicating even before there was language. Some historians believe dancing predates speech. One exercise would be for the class to pretend they are a tribe of cavemen sitting around the fire. One by one, each member gets up and "tells" the others about what has happened to him or her that day. Remember, these cavemen know no words. They may grunt, or make sounds, but they are not allowed to speak.

A second nonverbal exercise would involve the participants pretending they are from different countries and don't speak the same language. Each player needs to ask someone else a question or tell another person something. Since they don't speak the same language, words are not permitted. This exercise fits in well with the "Gibberish" concept discussed in the next section of this chapter.

Still another variation is for each person in the class to deliver a message either to one other person or to the class as a whole without speaking. Charade-type gestures are OK, but the player must remain mute until he or she gets the message across. (If it looks hopeless, the class leader may call a halt to the exercise.) For beginning level classes, it is usually necessary for the instructor or leader to supply the messages. In preparing for this session, write down some messages on slips of paper. As the students take the stage, they draw a slip of paper. Some sample messages might be: "I like you"; "I hate you"; "I am afraid"; "I have to leave soon"; "I am hot"; "I am cold." Keep the message simple. It is generally best to make the messages simple first-person declarations, like the examples listed above.

Most beginning actors are surprised to learn just how much information they can communicate without resorting to words.

Advanced improv groups might want to try the "Randomly Selected Characters" exercise nonverbally.

Gibberish

It is hard for most people not to verbalize in exercises like those described in the preceding section. And, to be complete, the voice plays an important role in nonverbal communication. Or perhaps megaverbal communication would be a better term. The tone of voice, the pitch, the volume, and any changes in any of these features can say a lot about what is going on within a person or character.

To concentrate on the nonverbal aspects of speech, it is useful to perform improvisation structures using gibberish dialog. Any improv structure that normally incorporates dialog may be used. The actors must not use recognizable words. They may only speak gibberish, or nonsense syllables.

Some actors take to gibberish dialog very easily. Others sometimes get hung up on the sounds they are making, and lose sight of the true goals of the improvisation. If members of your group seem to have problems in this area, encourage them to just repeat a nonsense phrase, such as "Ibba-dabba-foo-foo," throughout the improv with the proper inflections. Alternately, their dialog might be limited to numbers, or a single word, such as "umbrella," or "acorn." The sounds uttered are not important. They are intentionally meaningless. The entire meaning should come through the way the sounds are spoken, not the sounds themselves.

Almost any dialog improv structure can be used as a gibberish exercise. Perhaps the most obvious, and conceptually simplest format to use is one of the nonverbal communication exercises from the last section. The participants pretend that they are from different countries and don't speak the same language. Each player needs to ask someone else a question or tell another person something. Since they are supposedly speaking a foreign language, gibberish fits in very naturally. No actor should be permitted to use a language he actually knows, or he will start concentrating on the words. The foreign language does not have to be a real language. The speakers could be from Mars or Venus.

If an actual language, such as German or Japanese, is supposedly being used in the improv, it is still not necessary for the actors to try to imitate the sound of the actual language. More advanced actors may want to roughly approximate the sound in a simple way — for example, harsh guttural consonants for German, or a sing-song quality for Japanese. But even this is not necessary.

If you can get hold of any videotapes from the old "Your Show of Shows" TV program, it will be well worth your while to study them in class. Sid Caesar is a master of gibberish. He could convince you he was speaking almost any language. He has said that his "secret" for this ability is that he always was thinking what he was "saying" in English, while letting his mouth make whatever nonsense sounds it wanted. This trick, coupled with a good ear and a natural sense of mimicry permitted Caesar to simulate many different languages. As an improv exercise, the mimicry part is not important. If you just think of words while speaking in gibberish, you will find it pretty easy to simulate an unknown language, even if it doesn't quite sound like any known real language.

Truth or Lie

An actor gets on stage or in front of the class. He tells two short, simple stories. Preferably, each story should just be a sentence or two. They should be about two different events in the actor's life. Some examples might be: "I once visited the Grand Canyon"; "When I was six years old, I got caught stealing a candy bar"; "I once won a pocket radio in a contest"; "The last time I went camping, I got bitten by a snake."

The stories should not have any strong emotional connotations. They should be fairly neutral.

One of these two stories should be true, but the other should be a lie.

The rest of the group can then ask questions about either of the stories for a period of five to ten minutes. The actor must answer all questions. "I don't remember" is an acceptable answer. The answers about the true story must all be true. The answers about the lie story, of course, will be lies. The other members of the group are not permitted to ask which story is true, of course.

At the end of the question and answer period, the group votes on which story was true. The actor then tells them if they were right or not.

All acting is, in a sense, is lying convincingly. The trick is to convince yourself that the lies you are telling are true.

A good actor in this exercise will not only try to sound confident and convincing when lying, he will also try to appear a little evasive and unsure of himself when telling the truth.

Hidden Motivations

Throughout this book I frequently refer to motivation. Motivation is a vital element of any good scene. If the characters are not trying to accomplish something, they can't be in conflict with one another. Without conflict, there is no drama — just a very boring conversation.

Motivation is not something mystical or difficult to understand. Whenever we do anything at all, there must be something we want to accomplish, some goal we are striving for. Unless we want the activity to do something (even if it's only to relieve nervous energy), there is no point in making the effort at all.

Several of the improv exercises presented so far touch upon motivation.

Some motivations are simple and obvious. We sometimes say what we want directly. For example, in a scene where an employee asks his boss for a raise, it is quite possible that the employee's motivation is spelled out directly — he wants the boss to pay him more money.

Often in more interesting scenes, motivations may be more subtle. They may not be directly expressed. In fact, sometimes in real life people will conceal their motivations. Characters can do the same.

In the "Hidden Motivations" exercise, two actors play an improvised scene without directly referring to their motivations. Nevertheless, both actors must keep their motivations in mind at all times. The hidden motivations will affect what is said and done in the scene. The motivations are implied by the course of the scene.

The motivations should be supplied by the director, group leader or teacher. The motivations may be written on a piece of paper, or whispered in the individual actor's ear. In any case, no one should know what the motivation is except the director and the actor using the motivation.

Who the characters are and where the scene is taking place may be decided by the director or teacher, or they may be selected using the cards described earlier in the "Random Characters" exercise.

A typical "Hidden Motivations" scene is one I once participated in. In this scene there were two men. I'll call them A
and B for convenience here. A and B are partners in an unsuc-
cessful small business. A has gotten an offer that will give him
a hefty kickback if he can get B to sell out his share of the
business at a low price. B, on the other hand, wants to keep
the business running because he has secretly been having an
affair with A's wife. In the improvised scene, A and B discussed
whether or not to sell the business. A was pushing strongly
for selling, while B was highly resistant to the idea. Their true
reasons were never directly mentioned, but they fueled the
conflict, and made for a very strong scene.

What's It Used For?

Props, or objects, can often be helpful in creating an alternate reality on the stage. In improv performances, the use of
props is usually quite limited because there's no way to know
in advance what props to have on hand. With a little imagination, however, a handful of simple props can be used to repre-
sent countless objects. A prop does not have to be used for its
ordinary intended function.

In this exercise, the director, group leader, or teacher
provides a small, simple prop of some kind. (For best results,
try the exercise several times with a number of different props,
but concentrate on just one at a time.) The prop is passed from
actor to actor. As each actor holds the prop, he must do a brief
improvisation using the prop. Just a line or two is often all
that's needed. The idea is to utilize the prop.

Encourage the actors to come up with imaginative uses
for the prop. Some people will have difficulty getting past the
prop's intended identity.

Once I did this exercise with a plastic lily. Several people
used the prop as a flower of some kind. A couple of people
showed some cleverness in how they used the flower. One guy
played a corpse with the lily on his chest. Another actor portrayed a hippie trying to smoke the flower. Others in the group
were able to get past the flower image. They used the plastic

lily as a microphone, a quill pen, a dagger, and a musical instrument.

The further you can take your imagination, the better. It is interesting to note that even when my plastic lily was used in the most far-out applications, once the function was presented clearly to the audience (the rest of the group), it immediately accepted the prop's new identity without any problem.

Chapter Summary

This has been a rather long chapter. Don't rush to do all of the improv exercises described here. Take the time to get good at each one before moving on. For a group of ten meeting for ninety minutes at a time, working completely through this chapter should take at least five to ten sessions.

If you are pressed for time, it is better to omit some exercises than to race through everything too quickly. Pick and choose the exercises you think will be the most beneficial for your individual group, considering its goals, strengths, and weaknesses.

It doesn't matter at all what the story is about as long as the performers keep it going without faltering.

Chapter 3
SIMPLE IMPROV STRUCTURES

I say the improvisation structures are simple, but that may be a bit misleading. These structures have fairly simple rules. It can still be difficult to do them well in a performance situation.

These structures are good ones to start with because they are easy to learn. In most cases, much comedy is inherent in the structures. It would be hard to perform some of these structures so that they will not be funny. (I can't imagine why you would want to try.)

These improvisation structures are also classified as simple because the performer doesn't have to worry much about the dramatic elements discussed in Chapter 1. These structures are not really scenes in the dramatic sense. They can still be enjoyable.

Complaint Department

This is a fun structure that almost anybody can do. It is an excellent party game. It is a bit risky to use as a performance piece because the performers have limited control, especially over the length. The performer who gets most of the laughs probably won't even know why.

Two performers participate in "The Complaint Department." One serves as emcee, and, to a certain extent, as straight man. We will call the emcee Performer A. Performer B is sent out of the room where he or she cannot hear Performer A and the audience. The audience is asked to name some object. Performer B is called back into the performing area, and the actual scene begins.

Performer A is a clerk in a store's complaint department. Performer B is a dissatisfied customer trying to return the object selected by the audience. The gag here is that B doesn't know what he's talking about. The scene ends when B figures out what the object is.

This structure will work best if B makes assumptions, rather than playing "Twenty Questions." When the scene begins, B assumes he knows what the object is. Of course, he is just guessing, and is probably wrong. This is where most of the humor in this structure comes from.

Performer A will not directly indicate what the object is, but his responses to B's assumptions will serve as clues. If the scene is going on too long, A has the responsibility of giving more obvious clues.

For most of the structures I will describe sample scenes to give you a clearer idea of how the structures work.

Let's assume the object selected by the audience is a raincoat. The scene might run something like this:

A: May I help you?

B: Yeah. I want to return this.

A: What's wrong with it?

(NOTE: Complaint Department will almost always begin with these three lines, or some variation.)

B: Well, I couldn't figure out how to turn it on.

A: Well, good. Because you don't turn this on.

B: Should I have used batteries?

A: No. This item doesn't use any kind of power source.

B: Well, that's what I thought. So I was using it in the kitchen.

A: Are you a sloppy cook?

B: Well, a little. Why?

A: I was trying to figure out why you'd need something like this in the kitchen.

B: Oh. I guess most people would probably use this in some other room of the house.

A: Most normal people only use this product outside.

B: Well, I didn't like the way it looked when I put it on my car.

A: Good. It doesn't go on your car. Maybe you could put it on *in* your car, but not on it.

By this time, B should have figured out that the item is something worn outside. A few more lines should narrow it down further. Notice that B does not ask questions. He doesn't, for example, ask "Should I use it in the kitchen?" He makes the assumption and says he used it in the kitchen. The humor comes from the inappropriate assumptions. B inevitably comes across as a total idiot. He should not "play stupid." This structure should be played absolutely "straight." Performer A may use a few insulting one liners when B says something particularly ridiculous, but it will generally be much funnier to pretend to be perfectly serious about it all.

Because this structure is so simple and easy to explain to the audience, some performance groups may be tempted to use it as their opener. Starting your show with a "guessing" structure is risky. If the audience is already "hot" and ready to laugh, it will probably go over pretty well. But if the audience is not warmed up, they are likely to be indifferent to such a simple piece. One group I briefly worked with usually opened with two or three Complaint Department or Who Am I? (discussed next) scenes. Invariably, when the second or third round was introduced, several people in the audience would leave. The scenes usually got fairly decent laughs, but whenever people walk out when you say you are going to do the structure again, something is seriously wrong.

Who Am I?

This is another "guessing game" structure, similar to Complaint Department. It would probably be very unwise to use two such similar structures in a single performance. Again, because of the guessing nature of the structure, this is probably better as a party game than a performance structure.

Performer B is sent out of earshot. The audience decides upon a celebrity. Performer B is then called back in to play the part of this celebrity, without knowing who it is. Performer A offers indirect clues.

As in Complaint Department, the humor arises from inappropriate assumptions on the part of Performer B. For example, if the celebrity selected by the audience is the president, and B starts talking about the rock album he's just recorded, the incongruity is going to be funny.

Unfortunately, this structure tends to be even more limited than Complaint Department. There are just so many types of celebrities. There are far more types of objects. Even so, any "guessing game" structure is limited as a performance piece. If either performer falls down on the job or gets blocked in any way, the scene will run far too long, more than wearing out its welcome.

Shopping List

This is a simple improvisation structure that can be a fun "filler." It shouldn't run more than one or two minutes.

Before the improv, the emcee asks the audience to name a number of objects. Both common and bizarre objects should be included. These suggestions are written down.

Two performers now begin the scene. They carry on a conversation. Periodically the emcee calls out one of the objects on the list. The performers then have to work that object into the conversation as soon as possible. They should try to make the reference to the object as logical as they can. As soon as one object is mentioned, the emcee calls out the next item. At the end of the scene, the conversation should return to the original object. A stock line that will usually work is, "And that's why I needed the *(name object)*."

This structure doesn't sound like much when it is described, but it can really test the performers' ingenuity. Even more than most improv structures, this one demands fast thinking.

Part of a typical Shopping List improv might run like this:

Emcee: Motorcycle helmet.
A: What are you doing with that motorcycle helmet?
Emcee: Banana.

46

ₐ: That's where I keep my banana.

Emcee: Dirty sock.

A: Oh, I always keep my bananas in dirty socks.

Emcee: Fountain pen.

B: Well, I tried that. But I keep my fountain pen in my dirty sock too, so it got ink all over my banana.

Emcee: Alarm clock.

A: Don't you know how to get ink off a banana?

B: How?

A: You use an alarm clock.

Emcee: Clothespin.

A: An alarm clock blots up ink a lot better than a clothespin.

B: I'd imagine it would. Besides, you put a clothespin on a banana, it can make an awful mess.

And so on. As you can see, this improv structure tends to get very silly. But it's surprisingly fun.

Story-Story — Emo

The next three structures are closely related. They are all called "Story-Story," but each features its own individual variation. The Story-Story structures are roughly similar to the Group Story exercise described in Chapter 2, except the performers say more than a single word at a time.

This structure requires three or four performers, and an emcee. Fewer than three or more than four performers don't seem to work out very well.

One of the performers begins telling a story. The emcee serves as conductor, periodically changing the speaker from performer to performer. Each performer tells the story from his or her own assigned point of view. This causes the story to take some really bizarre turns.

In Story-Story — Emo, the improv begins with the emcee asking for several emotions from the audience. The category of "emotions" can be very loosely defined for the purposes of this improv structure. It is OK to accept states of mind or con-

47

ditions such as drunk, forgetful, or stupid, even though these aren't really emotions.

Each performer is assigned an emotion. When it is his turn to speak, he tells the story with his assigned emotion.

Be careful in assigning emotions that no two are too similar. This structure is one of contrasts. The more drastic the change from speaker to speaker, the funnier it will be. Some examples of combinations to watch out for include fear and paranoia, anger and jealousy, or greed and jealousy.

It doesn't matter at all what the story is about as long as the performers keep it going without faltering. The "plot" probably won't end up being too coherent. A good way to begin is "I was walking down the street the other day, and I saw —." Then continue with something appropriate to your assigned emotion.

The emcee indicates a change of speakers by clapping hands once and pointing. It is best to mix up the order. The change should be made in midsentence. The next speaker must pick up from the exact word where the previous speaker left off. Complete the sentence. The shift of thought patterns in midstream is what is funny in this structure.

As the improv progresses, each performer should be permitted to speak for a shorter and shorter time on each round. To end the scene, the emcee can indicate that two or more speakers start talking at once, until eventually all are talking in a crescendo of babble. Alternatively, the story can be taken to a logical conclusion.

The performers should remember that they are telling a story. Concentrate on specific incidents, rather than generalized editorializing.

It is also a good rule of thumb for the performers to avoid stating their assigned emotion directly. If your emotion is joy or happiness, don't say, "I'm so happy." Instead, act happy. Get the emotion across by your attitude and how the story evolves when you are telling it.

Story-Story — Genre

This is a variation on the Story-Story structure. Instead of emotions, each performer is assigned a movie or literary style, or genre. The genres are taken from audience suggestions. Typical genres might include a hard-boiled detective story, kung fu movie, documentary, or romance novel.

It is best to avoid accepting specific authors or directors. This narrows the style too much, and requires the performer to be very familiar with the writer or director in question. If you accept one, it will look bad if you reject another. So, even if you think you could do a good job with a suggestion of "Stephen King," the emcee should generalize the suggestion to "horror."

Other than the use of genres rather than emotions, this improv structure is the same as the last one.

Story-Story — Characters

This is a somewhat more complex variation of the basic Story-Story structure. This time each performer plays a specific type of character. The characters are not specific people, but general types. Actually, we are working with stereotypes here. For example, the story might be collectively told by a panel made up of a hick, a yuppie, a scientist, and a gangster.

Unless the performers are extremely versatile, it is probably best to preset the characters rather than basing them on audience suggestions. Perhaps the audience suggestions could be used to determine what the story is about.

Very advanced or daring groups might want to try this structure using celebrities instead of general stereotypes. Again, the celebrity played by each actor could be preset. If you are a group of real risk takers, you could accept suggestions from the audience to determine the celebrities.

There is no need to do actual impressions. The actor does not have to look or sound like the celebrity in question. If the actor is true to the celebrity's attitudes, the audience will accept the characterization. However, watch out if you happen to have one strong impressionist in your group. If one performer does an actual impression, it will look bad if the others don't follow suit. Establish and agree upon the rules the entire group will play by beforehand. I'd advise a ban on impressions if you are taking audience suggestions for celebrities. Someone is bound to get someone they can't do, and that can kill the entire improv. Improvisation always involves taking risks, of course. But be realistic. Don't take unreasonable risks.

History

This is one of my favorite improv structures. To be honest, I probably like it mainly because it is one I seem to be particularly strong in. As you try a number of improv structures, you will undoubtedly find that you have a definite flair for certain structures, while other structures may be more difficult for you.

In some ways, this structure is similar to Story-Story. Once again, we have three or four performers and an emcee/conductor. Things tend to get unclear in this structure if the performers play specific characters. They should all be generalized lecturers. They can be played slightly pedantic if you like, but in this particular structure who is speaking should not be allowed to overshadow what is being said.

The audience is asked to name an object. The panel then proceeds to lecture on the history of the object. Periodically, the emcee claps his or her hands and the speakers change. As in Story-Story, the changes should be made in midsentence. The next speaker must complete the thought. The interrupted sentence should be grammatically correct, even if it veers off in an entirely new direction. There should be as little hesitation in the change as possible. The impression should be that the entire panel is thinking with a single brain. This is why individualized characterization doesn't work in this structure.

For best results, your "history" of the object should cover several historical periods. Don't start too close to the present, or you may end up getting stuck with nowhere to go. Good periods to begin with are the caveman era, or ancient Greece or Egypt. For any period, work in some appropriate historical references. For example, if you are talking about ancient Egypt, the object could have been used to help construct the pyramids, or in the Middle Ages, it might have been taken along on the Crusades. Obviously, accuracy isn't too important. Some anachronisms can be funny. Whenever the cavemen are used, dinosaurs seem to enter the picture, even though the dinosaurs had all died out long before there were any human beings. Such factual errors never seem to bother the audience.

Be very imaginative in the uses of the object throughout history. If the object is a clothespin, don't have the cavemen using it to hang up their animal hide garments. The humor usually comes from wild, but semi-semi-logical possible uses. Perhaps the cavemen invented the clothespin to wear on their noses because of the smell from dinosaur droppings. Or it could have been used as a pinching weapon in the Crusades. (The image of knights doing battle armed with clothespins is certainly imaginative.)

When other performers are speaking, listen carefully. You don't want to repeat a use for the object someone has already mentioned. You also don't want to backtrack in the history. If someone has spoken about the Old West, you can't jump back to the Dark Ages. Keep the history moving forward.

It is particularly important to listen very carefully to the speaker immediately before you. The emcee could clap at any second and you must be prepared to begin speaking immediately. Don't try to preplan what you are going to say or you will inevitably get stuck when the emcee claps at a moment when you're not expecting it. It is best to go with a stream of consciousness flow. When it's your turn to speak, say the first thing that comes to mind that fits the sentence grammatically. The wilder your statement is, the better. Start speaking without hesitation. Worry about the statement making sense after you've said it.

The emcee should clap when the current speaker is in the middle of a sentence, especially when he or she seems to be going strong. A lot of the life in this improv structure comes from the performers' frustration when they are trying to build

51

up to a good joke and the emcee cuts them off. The
will probably change the direction of the history to
the speaker is faltering, obviously unsure of what t
the audience (and the performers) will be expecting t
to clap for a change of speakers. Try not to fulfill these expectations. If at all possible, force the faltering performer to be
creative and dig himself out.

The lecture should pass through the entire panel three
or four times. More than this will make the structure seem to
drag. When the emcee hears a good ending line, he or she
should give three quick claps to signal the performers. They
should then say in unison, "And that's the history of —." Of
course, the blank is filled in with the audience-suggested object.

If the lecture has moved up to the present without an
ending, the speakers can start talking about the prospects for
the future uses of the object.

Throughout this structure, it is strongly advised to avoid
sexual uses, especially in the early stages of the improv. Sex-
ually oriented jokes will tend to leave you nowhere to go (except
possibly further into the gutter). The scene will often lose
momentum after a cheap "dirty" laugh. As always, the line
between acceptable and unacceptable humor is an individual
judgment call. I just want to warn you that risqué material is
particularly risky in this improv structure.

Talk Show

This improv structure is more or less a parody of TV
shows like "Donahue" and "Oprah Winfrey." There are a
number of possible variations on this structure.

At least two performers are required. One is the "host,"
and the other is the "guest." You could use multiple guests,
but then the structure could evolve into the Panel Discussion
structure which is discussed next.

The guest fields questions from the host and from the
audience. Who the guest is or the topic under discussion may
be taken from audience suggestions, or they may be preset. If
they are preset, a few questions from the host and their answers

may be prewritten. Of course, questions from the audience will require improvised answers.

While there are many possible variations on the Talk Show structure, perhaps the best uses three performers. In this version, A is the host of the talk show. B is a foreign celebrity or authority of some kind. C is B's interpreter. B and C must be adept at speaking gibberish.

The basic pattern of this structure is as follows: A asks a question or repeats the question taken from the audience. C "translates" the question into gibberish for B. B replies in gibberish. C then "translates" B's response, which will usually be a punch line. The gibberish exchanges give C time to think up a good answer, besides being funny in themselves.

When speaking in gibberish, try to capture the sound of the language you are faking. This does not require any knowledge of the language in question, just a good ear. For example, German is harsh and guttural, while Oriental languages tend to be musical with an almost singing quality. If at all possible, get hold of some videotapes of the old TV program, "Your Show of Shows." Sid Caesar is the acknowledged master of gibberish and faking languages. One useful trick he says he uses is that he always is thinking of a specific line in English. He doesn't just babble. He acts like he is really saying something. This gives a very convincing illusion of a real language.

As some of the workshop exercises (Chapter 2) should have revealed, it is possible to communicate through gibberish. Performer B is not just a time filler. He or she can help Performer C, who carries much of the weight in this improv.

Extra comedy can be obtained by throwing in a few English words and gestures while speaking gibberish.

This structure may be very hard for some performers. Some people take to speaking gibberish very easily. Others never seem to get the knack of it.

Panel Discussion

This structure is very similar to Talk Show. Once again, the key performers answer questions from the audience. The cast of this improv consists of three to four "experts" and a host or moderator. The host takes the questions from the audience, and imposes some degree of order.

Each of the "experts" should have a distinct character, as different as possible from the others. This structure derives much of its humor from contrasts.

The best way to work this improv is to preselect the characters of the "experts." Before the improv, the audience is asked to determine the topic, probably some issue of the day. The characters will probably end up being inappropriate to the subject matter, increasing the humor.

Questions are taken from the audience. Each of the "experts" replies to the question in character.

Press Conference

This structure is yet another variation on the Talk Show and Panel Discussion. The difference is that only one performer is answering the questions posed by several other performers.

Three to six performers are reporters from various magazines. The magazines should be preselected. They should not be magazines that would ordinarily attend a press conference. *Time* or *Newsweek* wouldn't be funny. Instead, use publications such as *Soap Opera News, Popular Mechanics,* and *Boys' Life.*

One performer is on the "hot seat" as the person giving the press conference. The audience may select who this person is. You can either ask for a specific celebrity, or the speaker may be a representative from an audience-selected company or organization.

The reporters ask the speaker questions, which may or may not be appropriate to the speaker. The questions should be appropriate to the magazine. For example, the reporter might ask the speaker's opinion of a new model chain saw. The speaker must respond according to his or her position and point of view. This creates some very incongruous humor. The speaker must really carry much of the weight of this structure. This performer must be very quick at coming up with funny answers.

The reporters may predetermine certain questions appropriate to their magazine. Remember, the questions do not have to be appropriate to the audience-selected speaker. The speaker may or may not be forewarned about some of the questions, depending on how your group works best.

As an example, when I have used this structure, I have sometimes had the reporter from *Highlights for Children* ask "Can you find the bunny in this picture?" This question is followed by a quick blackout, ending the scene.

The Brain

The Brain is another structure in which the performers answer questions from the audience. Once again, there is a host or emcee to take the questions from the audience. The Brain is made up of three or four performers. The emcee introduces them as the world's leading authority on everything. These people share a single brain among them and it is the world's greatest brain. They will answer any question on any subject.

The Brain answers the questions collectively. Each performer speaks one word at a time. This part of the improv is similar to the workshop exercise, Group Story, discussed in Chapter 2. There should be no hesitation from word to word, or from speaker to speaker. You must maintain the illusion that the performers are thinking with a single brain. Say the first word that pops into mind that fits grammatically with what has gone before. The sillier the answers, the funnier the improv will be. The performers should not try to preplan what they'll say next. Because each performer has no control beyond a single word at a time, the odds are you won't be able to use what you've planned. When the collective answer doesn't go the way you thought it would, it can throw you off. You'll probably hesitate when it comes your turn to speak because you were planning to say something that no longer fits. It can take several seconds to clear your mind and come up with something that does fit. It's best to just go with the flow. Don't try to predetermine what will happen next.

A nice extra touch for this improv structure is if the performers making up The Brain use some sort of coordinated, or possibly even choreographed motions. If seated, they could all cross and uncross their legs in unison on certain cues. The beginning of an answer is a logical (and clear) point to cue a motion. The performers may be seated or they may stand in a row. Alternately, they may be staggered. This works best with a team of three. One performer, in the back, stands. The second sits in a chair directly in front of the first. The third performer sits on the floor right in front of the chair. When speaking, the performers can extend and wave their arms, giving the effect of a multiarmed god.

This structure is also known as The Oracle. Other than the name, there is no real difference in the structure.

The keys to success in this improv are to listen carefully to what is being said by the other performers (very important in all improv structures, but particularly vital here), go with the flow, and speak off the top of your head. Say the first word that comes to mind that fits the sentence. If it doesn't make any sense, that's OK.

Freeze Tag

A number of performers consider Freeze Tag to be "pure" improv. It is practically a freeform structure.

Two performers begin a scene. At some point, another performer in the group claps and shouts "Freeze!" The performers on stage hold their current positions as the third performer comes on stage. The newcomer takes the place of one of the original performers, adopting the same position. The performer who has been tagged out leaves the playing area. Now, a new scene begins based on the positions of the actors. The more drastic the change, the better.

For example, there could be a scene about two street sweepers. The actors mime holding their brooms before them. Another performer tags in, and the scene changes to two people on pogo sticks.

A good imagination and a strong ability to visualize are required for Freeze Tag.

This structure is usually one of the most exciting, both for the performers and the audience, because nobody can even begin to predict what will happen next.

Punch lines are particularly dangerous in Freeze Tag. If no one tags in, you may be stuck with no place to go in the scene after the punch line.

I'd like to offer an incidental word of warning. When this structure is introduced to the audience, the emcee should be very careful of the wording. It is easy to say "anyone can tag in." Make it clear that anyone *in the performing group* can tag in. I've seen people in the audience try to participate. Naturally, this is even more of a problem for performances in clubs where the audience has been drinking. In one performance, some guy in the audience shouted "Freeze!" at least half a dozen times. Fortunately, some of his friends held him back from going up on the stage. The moral is, make the degree of audience participation in an improv structure absolutely clear to the audience.

Chapter Summary

This chapter featured several easy to learn, but challenging improv structures. If your group practices just these structures, they will be able to put on many entertaining improv performances. For more adventurous groups, the next two chapters will present a number of more complex and sophisticated improv structures. Incidentally, you may find that some of the more complex structures are easier to do (once you learn them) than certain more simple structures.

Most character type improvs use two actors. The emcee will ask the audience, "Who are these people?"

Chapter 4
CHARACTER IMPROV STRUCTURES

The improv structures presented in Chapter 3 can be fun and challenging, and they can get a lot of laughs in performance. But as drama, or true scenes, they are a little weak. This is because drama (including comedy) is a form of story telling, and all good stories are about people, or characters.

In the preceding chapter, the improv structures did not place much emphasis on characterization or the conflict which is at the heart of all stories, drama, or scenes. Performing in such improv structures isn't really acting.

This chapter will discuss a number of true dramatic improv structures. They can be used in performance (or the classroom or workshop) to create either comic or seriously dramatic scenes.

Character Suggestions

In an improv performance, the actors could play predetermined characters in situational scenes suggested by the audience. Performers willing to take a bigger risk and open themselves up to true improvisation will also let the audience determine the characters they will play.

Most character type improvs use two actors. The emcee will ask the audience, "Who are these people?" Rather than naming specific individuals, the audience should be instructed to suggest types of people or occupations. For example, some good suggestions might be: wino, cop, street cleaner, poet, mother, alien being.

Sometimes audiences will shout out specific names of celebrities, such as John Wayne or Dr. Ruth. You should refuse all such specific identity suggestions unless your performance group consists solely of excellent and versatile impressionists

59

ready to portray any imaginable celebrity. You must be consistent about refusing such suggestions. If one of your actors does a few good impressions, it may be tempting to accept a suggestion for one of his impression specialties. Unfortunately, once you open the door, you'll find it very hard to close it again. If you take one celebrity suggestion and reject the next one, you're going to look bad. The audience will begin to doubt that you are truly improvising. Many people will assume that the other celebrity suggestion came from a plant in the audience.

To do a bad impression of a celebrity will generally result in a weak improv scene, and the audience probably won't enjoy it as much. And there's always the possibility that an actor will be assigned a celebrity role that he is completely unfamiliar with. For example, I have little or no interest in sports. If I had to portray a famous athlete, I'd be at a total loss. I could only play a generalized, nonspecific athlete, even if I used the name of a real athlete. I would not be able to capture any of the famous athlete's individual characteristics which the audience will be expecting.

Don't ask for trouble. The emcee should periodically remind the audience to keep the suggestions general. Ask for a type of person, not a specific individual.

There are several possible approaches to assigning audience-suggested characters to the actors in the improvised scene. You could take one suggestion for both; for example, two astronauts, or two waitresses. You could take separate, independent suggestions for the two characters, such as a truck driver and a priest. I think the best approach is to ask the audience to come up with a pair of related roles for the actors to play in the scene. The emcee can ask, "Who are these people? What is their relationship?" The relationship can be job related, or blood related, or any other type of relationship between the two characters. Some examples of good relationship suggestions are as follows: waiter and customer, mother and child, astronaut and alien, boss and secretary, teacher and student.

Location Suggestions

Every scene must take place somewhere. The location will very often affect the direction of the scene. For example, most characters would be expected to behave and speak differently in a church than at a race track.

Once again, the emcee should ask the audience for general rather than specific locations. For instance, a discount store instead of K-Mart.

When asked for a location, many audiences will tend to shout out names of cities such as New York, Phoenix, or Miami. Such suggestions are usually hard to work with. In some cases, a specific city suggestion may be useful. For example, Washington, D.C. will probably result in a scene about politics. Fictional or mythical settings such as the Land of Oz or hell, may also work. But generally, you are likely to get yourself in trouble with geographic locations.

One way around this kind of problem would be to get *two* location suggestions when necessary. For example, if the audience suggests "Boston," ask them for a type of place in Boston. A "fast food restaurant in Boston" will be easier to play than just "somewhere in Boston."

The emcee should explain to the audience that he is asking for general types of settings for the scene. Some good examples might include: a singles bar, a graveyard, a fashion boutique, a classroom, a golf course.

The actors should keep the scene environment in mind. What kind of activities might take place in that setting? What objects are likely to be present? Does your character belong in the setting, or does he feel out of place? If the character is in an unlikely setting, why is he there?

The Improv Structure

Back in Chapter 1, I identified four basic elements which are needed for a good dramatic scene (whether improvised or not). Remember, I am using the word "dramatic" in the sense of theatrical story telling. Purely comic scenes are included.

The four dramatic elements are: characters, setting, conflict and action, dialog (and humor, if a comedy).

In the character-oriented improv structures of this chapter, the first two of these elements are automatically included. The characters and setting are provided by the audience suggestions, at least in rough form.

Presumedly, the improvising actors will be saying something, so dialog will also be included.

The only element that might be missing is conflict and action. The improvising actors must come up with some kind of motivation. They should each want something which puts them into conflict with one another.

Once the improvising actors have motivated their characters and found a good, strong conflict, the scene will move along almost by itself. Much (hopefully most) of the dialog will come easily and naturally.

Each of the improv structures in this chapter are basically variations on one another. The foundation for all of this chapter's improv structures is covered in the Basic Character Improv, which will be discussed shortly.

Because these structures are in the form of true dramatic scenes, improvisations of this type tend to be fairly strong. These structures hold up to repetition better than the improv structures described in Chapter 3. You can repeat a character-oriented structure several times with each scene seeming to be totally different. The repetition will not appear redundant. Additional special elements in each variation of the Basic Character Improv can create considerable variety in the performance.

Some improv groups put on entire shows using only this type of structure.

Many, if not most, of the improv structures that were presented in Chapter 3 do not really require any acting, in the traditional sense. Nonactors may do as well as, and in some cases better than, trained actors.

Character-oriented improvs, on the other hand, require good acting. The performers must portray definite characters relating to one another as individuals. This is considerably similar to the type of acting done in a play. In fact, a good character improv is really a short play except that the script is created simultaneously with the performance, rather than being previously written down and memorized.

Because of the emphasis on character and dramatic form, the structures described in this chapter make excellent advanced exercises for acting classes.

This type of improv is often used to develop scripts. Sometimes a script will start out as a pure improvisation, and not be written down until after the scene has been improvised several times. Other times, improvisation can be used to carry an existing incomplete script beyond what has been written down so far.

Often, when directing a play from a published script, I will use some rehearsal time for the actors to improvise scenes not actually in the play. This gives them an opportunity to get to know their characters much more intimately.

Basic Character Improv

The Basic Character Improv is quite simple to describe. Two (or occasionally three in advanced groups) actors perform the scene. They play characters defined by the audience in a location also defined by the audience. The requirements for these audience suggestions were discussed earlier in this chapter. To recap, the suggestions should be general types, rather than specific individuals or locations.

The actors will then have to make decisions to make their characters and their environment believable. The characters are not patterned after any specific person, but they must seem like a real person. A mail carrier, for example, is not just a mail carrier. He is a *specific* individual who happens to work as a mail carrier. If the scene calls for two mail carriers, they should not be interchangeable. The audience suggestion is basic and general. The actor's job is to flesh out the simple suggestion into an actual character who serves the needs of the improvised scene.

In a very real sense, the Basic Character Improv structure is dramatic improvisation in its purest and most direct form. The actors are writing a playlet as they perform it. In most cases, the improvised scene will work best if it is in dramatic form. That is, the scene should tell some kind of story. Some improv structures (including most of those outlined in Chapter 3) can function without a dramatic story form, but a character improv almost always demands more than just witty lines.

Any story or dramatic scene ultimately is built upon some sort of conflict. There are many different types of conflict, but for our purposes here, we will just consider one type. In the improvised scene, we have two characters. For dramatic story form, these characters should be in conflict with one another.

Conflict grows out of motivation. Motivation is simply what a character wants. If he doesn't want anything, he has no reason to do anything. If he doesn't do anything, there is not only no conflict, there is no scene at all. An actor trying to play a character who doesn't want anything can only sit there like a lump.

The motivations of the characters are what cause all action in any scene. The motivation does not have to be a heavy, psychological concept. For improvised scenes, it is best to stick with more direct, conscious-level motivations. For example, Bob asks Jill for a date. Bob's motivation is to get to spend some time alone with Jill. This is pretty basic, and should be quite obvious. But without any motivation, Bob will not only not ask Jill for a date, he won't do anything at all.

Some motivations are very minor and momentary. As I was typing this paragraph, I paused to scratch the back of my left hand. I didn't do this randomly. I had a reason, or motivation, for my action. In this case, the back of my hand itched, and I wanted the sensation to stop, so I scratched my hand. That solved the problem, and the motivation vanished. It was a momentary, minor motivation.

To hold a scene together, the characters will need larger motivations. They don't have to be earth shattering. (They probably shouldn't be earth shattering.) But the character should want to accomplish something, and it should be something more significant than scratching himself. If each character has a main motivation, this will propel the scene very naturally. By main motivation, I do not mean a life-long quest. The character is focused on this motivation for the length of the scene. It doesn't have to extend beyond that. Generally, the action of the scene will lead to a resolution of one (or sometimes more than one) character's main motivation. Does the character get what he's after, or not? When the scene answers this question, you have a good strong ending. There is no point in going on with the scene after this point. The improv is over, and the audience will feel satisfied. If the scene just stops without resolving any questions, it will seem incomplete. The audience will feel cheated, and rightfully so. They did not get to see a complete scene — just a fragment of a scene.

Most improvised scenes of this type will involve just two performers. It actually gets harder to improvise a dramatically satisfying scene as more characters are added.

Dramatic Motivation

Dramatic motivations are best if they are specific, calling for a definite action. To return to the earlier example about Bob and Jill, it would be very difficult for the actor playing Bob to work from a motivation like, "I want Jill to like me." Instead, Bob should want Jill to respond in a definite way. Better motivations for Bob might be, "I want Jill to agree to go out on a date with me," or, "I want Jill to give me a kiss," or even, "I want Jill to say she loves me." These motivations are clear. Success or failure will be unmistakable and unambiguous. Either Jill says "Yes," or she says "No." Bob (and the audience) will know for sure if he has accomplished his goal or not. But how can we know if Bob has successfully gotten Jill to like him or not? Even if she agrees to the date, kisses him, or even says she loves him, that doesn't conclusively prove she likes him. She might perform any of these actions to fulfill some other motivation of her own. She might actually hate Bob. Choose a definite motivation that can be clearly fulfilled (or not fulfilled) with a specific action.

Each actor must select the necessary motivations for his character "on the fly." If you can learn how to quickly select a suitable motivation, the rest of the improvisation process should be a snap. If the character wants something definite, it is generally no trouble at all to think of things for him to say or do. He will be working toward a definite goal.

For dramatic scenes, the two characters should be in conflict. That is, they should have conflicting motivations. Character A wants x, and Character B wants y, which precludes x. That is, if Character B gets what he wants, that will prevent Character A from getting what he wants. Such a conflict will propel a scene in ways which will be dramatically interesting. Without such a conflict, there won't be much of a scene. Let's go back to Bob and Jill once more. Assume the following motivations: Bob wants Jill to go out on a date with him. Jill wants to go on a date with Bob. The scene will play something like this:

BOB: Jill, will you go out with me?
JILL: Sure, Bob.

The scene's over, and big deal. Even if the actors stretched it out some more, it wouldn't be very interesting. The ending is a foregone conclusion. There is no suspense, because there is no conflict.

But what if we used the following motivations for the same characters? Bob wants Jill to go out on a date with him. Jill wants Bob to fix her up with his brother Paul. Ah, now we have a conflict. How will the scene end? It's hard to predict. There are several possible endings. Because the ending is in doubt, there is suspense. The audience cares about what is going to happen next.

When the two characters have conflicting motivations, there are several possible endings. Some of the more obvious of these include:

Character A gets what he wants, and Character B doesn't.

Character B gets what he wants, and Character A doesn't.

Character A or Character B modifies his motivation, or changes his mind about what he wants.

Character A and Character B reach some kind of compromise.

The conflict escalates, and Character A or Character B attempts (or succeeds in) eliminating the obstacle presented by the other. For example, if Character A kills Character B, that certainly resolves the conflict.

The ending of the scene should resolve the conflict in some way. It should answer the question, "Who wins?" The answer may be "Character A," "Character B," or neither. In rare cases, the answer might possibly be "Both," but this kind of ending only works in a few special scenes. Usually it will be dramatically unsatisfactory because it denies the conflict. If both characters are able to get what they want, they weren't truly in conflict.

As you can see, the motivations of the two characters are interlinked. But in a performance improvisation, you don't, by definition, get a chance to preplan such details. This is why it is important for the improvising performers to rehearse together as much as possible. They need to know each other very well. A good improvisation team will give each other hints, and will work together in finding suitable motivations at the start of the scene. One or the other will take the lead at some point, and establish his motivation. If the second actor is paying attention, he will quickly pick up on his partner's motivation, and select a suitable conflicting motivation for himself. Sometimes there may be some miscommunication, so it is also vital for the first performer to be paying close attention to the second. If the second performer mistakenly selects a motivation that doesn't conflict, the first performer must modify his motivation accordingly. Good improvisation is a matter of give and take. Neither performer can be the "star" or "leader" of the scene. Either both performers work together, or they will fail together.

On a related note, an important rule of improvisation is

"Never deny." This rule is especially important in a character improv structure. Never say no to a statement of fact. If Character A says "What a lovely garden," then Character B should *not* say, "We're not in a garden, you idiot. This is my kitchen." Yes, Character B will probably get a laugh, but the cheap joke will totally destroy the reality of the scene. Because generally there is no scenery, and no costumes, and virtually all props are mimed, the only way for the audience to know what is going on is for the actors to tell (or show) them. If the actors don't agree on such matters, it will be impossible for the audience to care about the story they are trying to tell.

When I mention the "reality of the scene," I am not necessarily referring to realism as a theatrical style. Of course, an improvisation may be performed in any style, especially broad farce and absurdism, which are nonrealistic styles. But every scene must have its own reality. That is, the scene must be true to itself. In this sense, the word "reality" refers to the rules of the scene's world. These rules are implied, rather than explicit, but if they are violated, the integrity of the scene will be damaged. The audience will no longer accept the characters and their motivations, or care about what happens in the scene. If anything can happen, who cares what happens? It just doesn't matter.

Often it will happen that one performer will say something that gets in the way of where the second performer wanted to take the scene. Tough. The second performer must go with the flow of the scene. The inevitable surprises are what makes improv so exciting for both the performers and the audience.

If your partner in an improv scene introduces an element that you don't like, don't deny it. Instead of saying "No," say "Yes, and —." For example, if Character B feels a kitchen sink will be necessary, and Character A says, "What a lovely garden," there are several things Character B can do. Some possibilities include:

Character B can forget about the planned kitchen sink, and follow the scene in a new direction.

Character B can say, "Yes, it is a lovely garden. But let's go inside now. I want a glass of lemonade." This will move the scene into the kitchen without breaking the reality of the scene. A transition has been provided.

Character B can say, "I'm glad you like my garden. But I hate all this dirt. So I had a kitchen sink installed behind the rose bushes."

Yes, this is ridiculous, but the silliness does not break the reality of the scene. Improvisations often have absurd elements, and audiences usually accept them, as long as they don't contradict one another.

Don't deny. Never say "No." Say "Yes, and —." And you should certainly never deny another character's motivation. Do not, under any circumstances, say "That's not what you want," or any variation of this statement. This should be perfectly obvious, and it ought to go without saying. Unfortunately, I have seen just this sort of thing done in some performance improvisations. Of course, when this is done, the scene almost inevitably flops.

Cooperation is vitally important in all improv structures. Nowhere is this more true than in character improvs. If the performers don't cooperate and work together, there is almost no chance at all of the scene working. If one performer looks bad, both will look bad.

The Basic Character Improv is very versatile, and countless scenes can be created within this basic structure. A number of variations can be built upon the Basic Character Improv structure. A full show could be staged using nothing but character improvs, without seeming repetitious. The remainder of this chapter will describe several variations on the Basic Character Improv.

Changing Emotions

Of course, emotions are important in any dramatic scene. In the Changing Emotions Character Improv, emotions are manipulated to create an absurd effect. The results are almost automatically and inevitably funny. This is one of the few improv structures that could be considered almost fail proof, assuming, of course, the performers are competent and don't allow the scene to fall apart.

As in the Basic Character Improv, this structure begins with the emcee asking the audience to define who the characters are, and the setting for the scene. The emcee also asks the audience for a list of emotions and states of mind. Some examples might be: fear, joy, anger, despair, confusion, lust.

The list should include a dozen or so items of this type. The emcee does not have to directly reject any inappropriate or undesired suggestions. The entire list won't be used anyway.

Once the emcee has finished collecting the needed information from the audience, the two performers take the stage and begin a scene, just as in an ordinary Basic Character Improv. From time to time, the emcee, who is standing in the wings or off to one side of the stage, shouts out one of the emotions from the list. The two performers must then immediately go into the specified emotion. The faster they can make the changes, the funnier the effect will be. Sudden reversals will usually get the biggest laughs. For example, if the last emotion was anger, one character might be saying, "I hate you! I hate you! I hate you!" The emcee calls out, "Joy." The character continues, now saying, "Oh, it's so much fun to hate you!" And the other character replies, "Yes! I love it when you hate me." This kind of thing is much funnier on stage than it might seem from just reading it.

For the best results, the emcee should be well rehearsed with the performers. Which emotions are added will be the biggest factor in determining the audience's enjoyment of the scene.

The actors should not directly refer to the specified emotion. If the emcee shouts out, "depression," neither actor should say "Gee, I'm so depressed." The audience will feel cheated if you take such an easy way out. Instead, the actors should let the audience see the characters' sudden nose dive into depression. There is an old adage that appears in almost all books

70

and lectures on creative writing — "Don't tell, show." Remember, in an improvisation, the actors are, in effect, writing their script as they go along, so the same rule applies. Don't tell the audience what the character is feeling. Show them.

An obvious variant form of this structure is to have the two performers working with different emotions. This has been suggested in a number of improv groups I've worked with. For some reason, this tends to become awkward. For less experienced groups, I'd advise that this structure be performed with both characters using the same emotions simultaneously.

If you do elect to use separate emotions for the two characters, there are two basic approaches you can take. The actors can alternate responding to the emotions called out by the emcee. Only one character responds to each new emotion. For example, the scene begins, and the emcee calls out the following list of emotions. The emotions are adopted by the characters as notated: irritability, Character A; dreamy, Character B; lust, Character A; revulsion, Character B; fear, Character A; rage, Character B; boredom, Character A; joy, Character B.

This system can work, but it is difficult. The actors have to concentrate on keeping the scene going, and they also have to keep track of whose turn it is.

Another approach is to use two emcees (probably on opposite sides of the stage). Each emcee calls out an independent list of emotions. Each character responds only to those emotions called out by his individual emcee.

To make this system work, select emcees with very distinctive voices. Make it as easy for the actors as possible. The scene could fall apart if the actors get confused over which emcee said what. It would probably be simplest if one emcee was a woman and the other was a man. The actors will then be able to tell who's speaking very easily, without having to exert much mental effort on this part of their improv task.

Besides the inherent difficulties involved in running the scene with the characters using separate emotions, some of the inherent humor may be lost. It is openly ridiculous for both characters to suddenly jump into a new emotion for no apparent reason. In most improvs of this type, one performer or the other will take temporary dominance when each new emotion is called out. The performers will almost instinctively take turns in dominating each emotion. The suggestions for separate emotions in this structure are usually based on the worry that the scene will become too mechanical and the characters too much alike if they are both following the same emotions at the same time. But in actual practice, this is rarely much of a problem. Assuming the performers are reasonably good improvisational actors, each will treat each emotion a little differently. The scene will almost always have the necessary dramatic contrast. Experiment with separate emotion variations if you like, but don't worry that they'll be necessary. They won't be. In my experience, they are rarely much of an improvement.

The Changing Emotion Improv may seem complex and difficult, but it really isn't. Once you have the basics of performance improvisation down, this one actually turns out to be a fairly easy structure. Changing Emotion scenes almost seem to play themselves as long as you take care of the basics.

Changing Styles

The Changing Styles Improv structure is very similar to the Changing Emotions structure described above. The emcee, as always, begins by asking the audience, "Who are these people, and where are they?" Then, instead of a list of emotions, the emcee calls for a number of theatrical or movie styles.

Genres are good. Some workable examples include: western, gangster film, TV game show, monster movie, soap opera, documentary, historical epic, slasher film, war movie.

The list may also include specific playwrights and film directors, but you will have to be careful here. Some are widely enough known, and easy to parody in an improvisation. Some good names include: Shakespeare, Harold Pinter, Beckett, Ibsen, Alfred Hitchcock, Disney.

But for the structure to work, the audience, and especially the actors, must be familiar with any name used. And even if you are familiar with the director's or playwright's work, some do not have a particularly distinctive style, or at least not one that can be easily caricatured. This is especially true of writers and directors who work primarily in comedy. How can you parody Neil Simon or Mel Brooks?

The emcee must use considerable judgment in selecting entries from the list. He must know the actors (and their film and theatrical knowledge) very well. The emcee should never play "stump the performers." Similarly, if the audience as a whole has a "Who?" reaction to a name suggested by one audience member, the emcee should probably not use it.

The emcee should not directly refuse any audience suggestions. The list approach makes this unnecessary. "Bad" suggestions don't have to be written down. If they are written down, they still don't necessarily have to be used.

The actors begin the scene as if it was a Basic Character Improvisation. Periodically, the emcee will call out one of the items from the list. The actors must continue the scene, but immediately revert to the appropriate style. Like the Changing Emotions structure, this improv structure can be quite funny even if the performance is just competent. The abrupt jumps from style to style is inherently funny.

Of course, in a gangster film, the characters should become gangsters (or perhaps a gangster and a cop). Their relationship remains the same, and the conversation should flow from what was said before, but changing the style changes the rules. The characters now talk (and think) like gangsters.

Similarly, a western would call for cowboys (or perhaps an Indian) to talk and act like their stereotypes, and in a slasher movie, the slasher would be demented. Teens would be "teens," for all that's worth.

Some people might think Shakespeare would be hard to do, but this is actually one of the easiest styles for this structure. Just use a lot of high-flown, pseudo-poetic phrases, and old English. Throw in some "thous" and "haths" and "doests" and much of the "Shakespearian" feel will come almost automati-

73

cally. Of course, any appropriate references to real Shakespeare plays will add to the fun.

As an example, let's say the actors are currently doing a gangster movie. A small snatch of the dialog might run like this:

CHARACTER A: You're the dirty rat who killed my brother.
EMCEE: Shakespeare!
CHARACTER B: Alas, poor Yorrick, I knew him well.
CHARACTER A: Verily, my goodly brother Yorrick now lies
    amouldering in the grave. Now, I seekest revenge.
CHARACTER B: What plannest thou, knave?

and so forth.

The Changing Emotions and the Changing Styles improv structures are a lot easier than they sound, and they are a lot of fun. These two structures are among my favorites. Audiences always seem to like them too.

Stop-Start

Stop-Start is a challenging and fun improv structure which depends heavily on the emcee. In this particular structure, the emcee is almost more important than the actors. If the emcee falls down on the job, the improv won't work well.

As with all of the structures discussed in this chapter, this improv features two actors. The emcee asks the audience, "Who are these people, and where are they?"

The actors begin the scene as if this was a Basic Character Improv. At some point the emcee will shout, "Stop!" The actors freeze, and the emcee asks the audience a question about what will happen next. Once an answer has been obtained, the emcee says "Start." The actors resume the scene according to the question asked and its answer.

For example, if one of the actors is about to open a box, the emcee will say, "Stop! All right, what's in the box?" Someone in the audience will shout up a suggestion. If more than one suggestion is called out, the emcee must select the suggestion that will be used. By improv etiquette, this ought to be the first suggestion heard, unless it is inappropriate or unusable for some reason.

Suggestions might be rejected because they are obscene or otherwise offensive. Occasionally, audience members may shout up "suggestions" that have nothing to do with the question asked. This most often occurs in a performance area where the audience is drinking. For example, if the emcee asks, "What's in the box?" he would not accept a shout of "Go to sleep" or "New Jersey" as the suggestion to work with.

But there is nothing at all wrong with accepting a totally bizarre suggestion. It might be logically inappropriate, but as long as it is semantically appropriate (a noun when a noun is called for, a verb when an action is called for, and so on), it can be used. It would be ridiculous if the actor was miming a small box, and the item contained in it was an elephant. But such silliness is part of the fun of improvisation. Now the actors must explain just why an elephant is being kept in a box. They may decide to play the scene as if it were a miniaturized elephant, or they may assume it is a full-sized elephant, without explaining just how it fit into the box in the first place. In either case, the elephant is now part of their scene.

In any event, the emcee should loudly and clearly repeat the accepted suggestion to make sure everyone, especially the actors, knows what it is.

The success of this structure is very heavily dependent on the questions the emcee asks the audience. They should not be too far out. Keep them appropriate to the scene. For example, if the scene is taking place in a department store, the emcee should not say, "Stop. OK, now they're on a rocket ship. Where are they going?" That has nothing to do with the scene. It is inappropriate, and it is cheating.

The emcee's questions should also be structured to limit the answers somewhat. The shorter the required audience response the better. Questions that can be answered "yes" or "no" are usually good. In this case, the audience as a whole may vote on the selected answer. Other questions should call for answers of one or two words. Some good questions might be: What is in the box? Does he believe what she just told him? Is the door locked? The phone rings — who is calling? Does she like that idea? Does A hit B? Is B hurt? Where does he want to go on their honeymoon?

It would be a bad idea to freeze the actors in a silly pose, and then ask the audience what they are doing now. The emcee should also avoid "Why?" questions. Bad choices for questions in this structure might be: Why does he want to leave? What happens next? What are they doing now? Why can't he open that jar? Why doesn't she like him?

The emcee's job is to keep the scene on track. He should not ask questions that are too open-ended, or that are unrelated to the scene. Bizarre and silly is fine. Inappropriate, disconnected nonsense will almost certainly flop.

Object Select

Object Select is a Basic Character Improv with a few audience-selected "props." Of course, these "props" are mimed by the actors.

After determining who and where the characters are, the emcee asks the audience to name a few (three is a good number) unrelated objects. It might be a good idea to ask for the objects separately, or the audience may call out related items. For instance, if the first suggestion is "pencil," there is a strong chance that the next suggestion will be "paper." This structure works best when the items are not logical combinations.

One way to avoid such automatic connectedness is to ask for each item separately with a slightly different question. For example: Name an object too large to carry; name an object that will fit in a pocket; name an object that makes some kind of sound.

By asking differing questions rather than just asking for three objects, you will break up the audience's train of thought. The objects are likely to be quite varied.

Another trick is to ask for object #1 while looking towards one section of the audience, then turn to another section of the audience for a suggestion for object #2. Physical separation of the people making suggestions also seems to minimize logical connections between the suggestions.

The actors then perform an ordinary Character Improv scene, except they must work the suggested objects into the action of the scene. Obviously, the more mismatched the objects are, the more challenging the scene will be, and the more wacky the humor will be. A scene involving, for example, a baloney sandwich, a hand grenade, and a typewriter is sure to be pretty wild.

Reversal

Reversal is probably the toughest of the character improv structures. It begins like an ordinary Basic Character Improv. The audience is only asked for who and where the characters are.

Periodically, during the course of the scene, the emcee will give a signal. This could be a loud, clear hand clap, or perhaps a shout of "Reverse!" The actors must now jump to an opposite point of view. If for example, Character A has been trying to get Character B to leave, after the call of "Reverse!" Character B will now want to leave, and Character A will try to get him to stay.

Both characters don't need to change on every reverse. Sometimes only the character speaking when the "Reverse!" call is made needs to reverse himself. For example: "I hate you! I hate you!" "Reverse!" "I love you! I love you!"

This structure is only recommended for experienced improv performers. It can flop big if it is not done right. But if it is well done, the results can be hysterically funny.

Chapter Summary

The improv structures in this chapter emphasize character, motivation, and plot. In addition to being very entertaining, they also make great acting exercises for classes, especially

77

the Basic Character Improv. The character improv structures calling for unexpected changes during the course of the scene (Changing Emotions, Changing Styles, Stop-Start, and Reversal) can be used to sharpen a student actor's concentration.

These improv structures are strong enough that an entire show may be made up of performances of just these types of improvs. The audience will be well satisfied if the improvised scenes are well done.

If you intend to later build up scripted (or semiscripted) scenes from your improvisations, you should certainly concentrate on character improvs because they lead to the best self-standing scenes. Some of the improv structures in Chapter 3 only work because they *are* improvisations and the audience gets to participate. As a prepared scene, these structures may not work very well. Many of them would be rather pointless. But a character improv is a miniplay, so it will work either as an improvisation, or as a prepared piece.

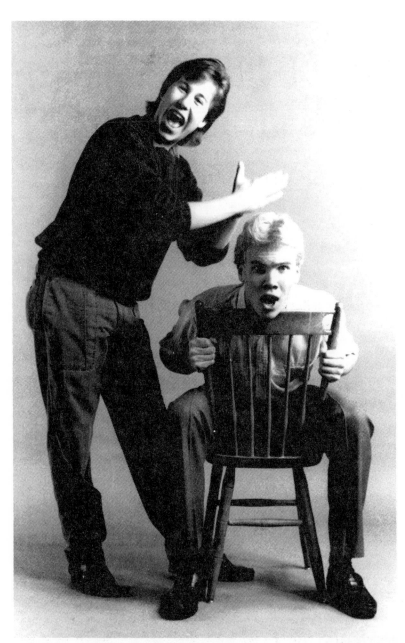

In playing "Double Emotions," the performers must make a credible transition from the beginning emotion to the ending emotion.

Chapter 5
ADVANCED IMPROV STRUCTURES

The improv structures discussed in this chapter are somewhat more complicated and difficult than those presented in the earlier chapters of this book. They call for more from both the performers and the audience. The rules for these structures are generally more complex.

In many cases, these structures call for more sophisticated audience participation. They are particularly difficult to pull off in a bar or other performance environment where the audience has been drinking.

Of course, for the audience to understand what its part is, the emcee will need to do a more thorough explanation before each improv is performed.

The performers need to be even more alert and "on their toes" to succeed with these advanced improv structures. They will generally have more details to keep track of.

For all their difficulties, these advanced improv structures can be extremely rewarding. Many performers find the challenge invigorating. When these structures are well done, most audiences seem to appreciate the extra effort too.

Fill in the Blank

The improv structure known as "Fill in the Blank" is relatively simple in concept, but it is rather difficult to perform well. You should be very well rehearsed in this structure before you attempt to do it on stage.

Basically, this structure consists of nothing more than two people holding a conversation. But they are very forgetful people. They often forget words and need the audience to help them out.

As one of the performers is talking, he'll hesitate and say "-uh- -uh- -uh- . . ." A consistent hand gesture of some sort will also help to cue the audience. The audience shouts up suggestions to fill in the blank. The performer repeats one of these suggestions and continues the sentence as if that was exactly what he meant to say in the first place.

Improv etiquette says that you should use the first acceptable audience response you hear. Do not be too picky. The audience will be disappointed and will suspect you're cheating. If you reject several responses, it is natural for the audience to assume that the response you finally do accept is probably from a prearranged plant. They will stop believing you are really improvising, and the performance will lose its point.

For a response to be acceptable, it should grammatically fit in the blank. That is, a noun where a noun is required, or a verb where a verb is called for. I once had the misfortune of performing this structure before an audience that had been drinking. One group kept shouting up "North Carolina" for everything. It almost never made any sense.

It is also all right to reject any obscene or offensive suggestions. If you intend to do this (and I advise it, or you'll end up getting nothing but blue suggestions), it is a good idea to inform the audience of the ground rules at the start of the show. Remind it again before you start the Fill in the Blank structure. You don't have to get preachy. Just say something like, "Let's keep it clean, folks."

Other than that, the audience should be encouraged to make its responses in this structure as wild and off the wall as it likes. This scene is supposed to be silly.

Here is an example of how this improv structure might run. Audience responses are in all capitals:

1. The other day I went down to -uh- -uh- -uh- . . .
   THE JUNKYARD
1. . . . the junkyard, and I was rummaging around the trash like I do every weekend.

2. Yeah, that's always a lot of fun.

1. And, you'll never guess what I found.

2. I'll bet it was a -uh- -uh- -uh- . . .

   BEAVER

1. No. I wish I had found a beaver. You can never have enough beavers. No, what I found was one of those -uh- -uh- -uh- . . .

   DIRTY SOCKS

1. . . . one of those dirty socks.

2. Oh, it's too bad you didn't find a beaver *and* a dirty sock. Then you could have -uh- -uh- -uh- . . .

   HAD A PICNIC

2. . . . had a picnic.

1. Oh, what I'd give for a good, old-fashioned beaver and dirty sock sandwich.

2. Yeah. That's almost as good as a sandwich made with -uh- -uh- -uh- . . .

   PENCILS

2. . . . pencils.

1. Yum! That's one of my favorites.

and so on.

As you can see, the performers more or less take turns providing blanks for the audience to fill in. The conversation is rather free form, going off in whatever direction the audience responses might suggest. For example, the picnic suggestion carries the conversation into eating.

The sillier this scene is, the better it will play.

Man on the Street

Man on the Street is a variation on the Fill in the Blank structure discussed above. The main difference is a tighter, more controlled format.

As the title suggests, this improvisation is set up as one or more "man on the street" interviews. One performer acts as the interviewer, serving primarily as the straight man for the bit.

The interviewer sets up the situation. He tells the audience that he is interviewing strangers. It helps to set the scene on a well-known street in the town where you are performing.

A second performer enters as if he is walking down the street. The interviewer stops him and asks the question of the day. A good general, open-ended question is "What's your beef?"

The passer-by replies with hesitating blanks, as in the Fill in the Blank structure. For example, "I'm sick and tired of all those -uh- -uh- -uh- . . ."

The audience shouts up suggestions to fill in the blank.

There are several advantages to this structure over the straight Fill in the Blank format. The interviewer has more control over the situation. Only the person being interviewed offers blanks for the audience to fill in. The interviewer can react to the absurdity of what is being said, heightening the humor. Several different people can be interviewed, one after another. As a rule of thumb, three is a good number. When one bit has run its course, or if it is leading nowhere, the interviewer can terminate the interview at any time, saying something like, "Well, thank you for your time. You've certainly given us all something to think about. I think I see someone else coming along now. Excuse me, sir —," And he goes right into the next subscene with a new partner. A single interviewer should be used throughout the structure.

Each of the interviews should be kept short — no more than a couple of minutes.

Besides the inherent silliness of Fill in the Blank, this structure gets a lot of humor by the interviewer's reactions to the strange people he is talking to. He knows what the other person is saying is ridiculous. The person being interviewed acts like he thinks he's being perfectly rational.

Double Emotions

At the start of the Double Emotions (or Double Emo) structure, the emcee asks the audience for four different emotions. For example: fear, joy, lust, anger.

For convenience, we will label the four audience-selected emotions A, B, C, and D.

Two actors are then brought up on stage. The emcee asks the audience who these people are, and where the scene will take place, as in the Basic Character Improv (see Chapter 4).

Performer 1 starts out in emotion A, and Performer 2 begins the scene in emotion B. At the end of the scene, Performer 1 should be doing emotion C, and Performer 2 should be in emotion D. The improv is over when both actors have completed their emotional transition.

This structure is not to be confused with the Changing Emotions structure described in Chapter 4. There, the point was to derive humor from rapid (and unmotivated) alterations of the character's moods. In the Double Emotions structure, on the other hand, the goal is for each performer to make a smooth and credible transition from the beginning emotion to the ending emotion. The better motivated the mood swing, the better the scene will play.

This structure really tests the performer's improvisational abilities.

Time Machine

The Time Machine structure is fun, but it is rather complicated and difficult to explain. The emcee's introduction to this structure must be carefully thought out or the audience won't be able to figure out what is going on. If the audience does not fully understand the structure, there won't be much point to the improv. The audience certainly won't be able to enjoy the performance if it is busy trying to puzzle out the structure.

This structure calls for an emcee and six performers. The emcee may double as one of the performers. The emcee's function is to explain the structure to the audience.

The structure starts out like a Basic Character Improv (see Chapter 4). Two actors are on stage. The emcee invites the audience to suggest who and where these people are. The performers now do a scene based on these suggestions. All other aspects of the scene are completely open-ended and up to the actors. The only restriction is that they cannot do a scene in which their characters are meeting for the first time. Essentially, these two performers are just doing a straight-forward Character Improv scene.

The scene may either play itself out to a natural conclusion, or the emcee may stop the scene at some point he deems appropriate. The first two performers leave the stage, and two different actors now take their place.

The emcee tells the audience that these new actors will be portraying the same characters as in the last scene, but at some earlier time. Obvious choices for the past scene are to act out the characters' very first encounter with one another, or the two characters may be portrayed as children. This scene may take place at any time in the characters' past. The only restriction is that it must occur before the "present" scene just performed by the first two actors.

When this "past" scene reaches a natural conclusion, or is stopped by the emcee, these performers leave the stage and are replaced by two more actors. The emcee tells the audience that these performers will now portray the same characters at some point in the future.

Generally, the Time Machine structure works best if the "future" scene is short, quickly reaching a strong and definite punch line.

The "past" and "future" actors have an advantage in this structure. They can consult with one another about what they are going to do during the "present" scene (and, for the "future" performers, during the "past" scene too). But they should not get so involved in preplanning that they neglect to watch what is happening on stage. The more tightly the three scenes are interwoven, the better the Time Machine structure will play. The "past" performers, for example, should refer to subject matter brought up in the "present" scene. It is especially good, if the "past" scene somehow explains some element of the "present" scene. For instance, if during the "present" scene, the performers refer to Character A's pronounced limp, the "past" scene might present the characters as children having an argument. Character B kicks Character A in the shins. Character A cries out, "Ouch! I'll never be able to walk again!"

Similarly, the "future" scene should refer back to the "past" and "present" scenes as much as possible. To continue the above example, the "future" scene could have Character A showing Character B his new crutch, and then hitting him with it. Now, Character B limps. For an even more bizarre touch, this could magically cure Character A's limp.

This structure is rather tricky, but if done well, it can steal the show. A good Time Machine sequence can be one of the strongest improvs you can do.

Foreign Film

Foreign Film is a totally silly improv structure. It may be semiprepared in advance.

In this structure, the audience is only asked to select a film genre. There are a few basic genres that will come up time and again, such as murder mystery, monster movie, or western. You could have a few stock "plots" worked up in rehearsals that you can call on when appropriate. Of course, you should keep yourself open to go off on new improvisational tangents. But you can provide yourself with a semiscripted "safety net" for this improv structure.

The number of actors is pretty variable, but six seems to work the best.

The point of this structure is to simulate a badly dubbed foreign film. Three of the performers are the physical actors in the movie. The other three performers provide the voices for the first three.

Different improv groups work this type of structure in two basic ways. Some position the voice performers where they have a good view of the action performers. Other groups prefer to deliberately place the voice performers where they cannot see the action performers at all. Either approach will work, although the overall effect of the scene will be quite different in either case.

When the voice performers can't see the action going on, some additional humor can be derived from incongruities between the dialog and the action. For example, once when I performed this structure, one character told another to "hold this." Because this was a gangster film, the action performers mimed a large gun. But then one of the voice performers said that the object being held "sure looked like a yummy ice-cream cone."

As a second example, two characters are fighting. A hits B in the stomach. B doubles over. B's voice says, "Ow! I think you just broke my nose!" A and B exchange looks, shrug, and A now hits B in the nose. And A's voice says, "I didn't mean to hit you in the face." This all sounds pretty stupid in print, but it can be surprisingly funny on stage.

On the other hand, when the voice performers can watch the action, a more coherent scene may be played out.

Most improv structures work best with two characters, but for some reason, three characters work better for Foreign Film. Three characters can cover more of the stereotypes of various film genres, and permit entrances and exits.

Watch out that you don't fall into the eternal triangle rut. If there are two men and one woman, there is a strong tendency to have the guys fighting over the woman, or if there are two women and one man, the women are likely to argue over him. This is OK once in awhile. Most film genres incorporate love stories, and jealousy helps motivate the action. But try not to get too repetitious.

I would not recommend using more than one Foreign Film scene in any one performance. This structure can be funny, but it can get old and wear out its welcome very quickly.

Do It Yourself Late, Late Show

This improv structure is sort of a cross between the Foreign Film structure discussed above, and the Stop-Start structure presented in Chapter 4.

Basically, the actors present a spoof of some specific film genre (monster movie, war film, weepy love story, or whatever). Periodically, the emcee stops the action and asks the audience to make some decision on what will happen next.

As in Stop-Start structure, the emcee's questions should call for short and simple answers from the audience. Some examples include: Does she believe him? Does he go with her? What is in the bag? Can he lift it? Does the key fit? The phone rings. Who is calling?

More than two performers may be included in this structure.

Personally, I like to work with a preselected genre, with a plot that has been partially worked out in rehearsals. At the start of the scene, the audience gets to cast the film. Generally, I start out with three stereotyped characters for the genre being spoofed. For instance, a monster movie could begin with these three characters: the mad scientist, the deformed assistant, the mad scientist's innocent fiancée. The audience votes on who among your improv troupe will portray each of these roles.

As the scene progresses, additional characters may be called for. The other actors in the troupe may jump in as any appropriate additional character. For example, the characters listed above might make references to the fiancée's father. One of the other performers in the group could enter the scene as the father.

As a rule of thumb, keep these additional characters in minor roles. They should not take over the scene. Let the performers cast by the audience be the "stars."

Three Person Freeze Tag

Freeze Tag was discussed in Chapter 3. It is freeform improvisation. Two performers are on stage doing a scene. The other actors in the troupe stand off-stage (or at the sides of the stage) watching. At some point one of them yells "Freeze!" The current actors hold their present positions. The performer who yelled "Freeze!" takes the place of one of the actors. The replaced actor leaves the main playing area. The two actors now on stage begin a new scene based on what their "frozen" positions look like. Each individual "scenelet" should be relatively short.

Freeze Tag calls for intense concentration, strong imagination and fast reflexes from all the performers in your improv troupe.

Advanced improvisers may attempt Three Person Freeze Tag. This is basically the same structure, but there are only three participants: the two actors performing the current scene, and one off-stage performer. The off-stage performer yells "Freeze!" and replaces one of the other two for a new scene. The pressure is really on the off-stage performer. He *has* to jump in. He can't wait and rely on someone else getting an idea. If he lets the scene drag on too long, the improv will fail.

Strong improvisers often love the challenge of this demanding structure. But let me caution you not to attempt it before an audience until you have a lot of experience, both individually and as a group. Get good at regular Freeze Tag first.

Sound Effects Story

In a Sound Effects Story, the audience is encouraged to provide appropriate sound effects.

At the beginning, the emcee asks the audience for several pieces of information, such as: a location, a small object, something that makes a sound, an animal.

These items will be worked into the scene. This part of the structure is somewhat similar to Object Select, which was presented in Chapter 4.

Generally, this structure will work best if the basic plot is more or less prearranged. For example, you could use a stock love story or detective story. The challenge to the performers in this structure is to work in all of the audience-selected items, and to provide ample opportunities for the audience to create sound effects. Usually one of the characters in the scene will also narrate the story (in the first person). Throw in lines like: It started to rain; I slammed the door; the traffic was terrible; I ran up the stairs.

Audiences seem to have great fun making sound effects. Because this structure tends to get the audience rather rowdy, it is best to use it as a finale for a show, or just before an intermission. Otherwise, some audience members might continue making sound effects during your next scene where that might not be appropriate, and may even be intrusive.

Chapter Summary

These advanced improv structures work on several levels at once. The actors have more things they need to keep track of. Often the audience must provide more sophisticated participation too. You will need a bright, cooperative audience to succeed in these structures.

Do not include too many advanced structures one after the other in a single performance. You will exhaust both the performers and the audience. Intersperse these structures with simpler improvs, and/or prepared scenes. Chapter 8 covers the scheduling of an improv show.

In "Voiceless Acting," each actor must portray his character and motivations solely through body language and facial expression.

Chapter 6
ADVANCED ACTING EXERCISES

In the last three chapters, we have been concentrating on improvisational structures for performance in front of an audience. Now, let's return to the workshop and classroom.

Since each of the performance improv structures makes specialized demands on actors, almost any of them could be used as acting exercises, especially the character-oriented structures of Chapter 4. Determine what you or your group needs to work on, and select an improv structure that emphasizes that particular element.

Of course, a teacher or workshop leader should feel perfectly free to modify any of these improv structures as necessary to create the desired learning experience.

This chapter will explore some improv structures specifically designed for the classroom or workshop. Modify these suggestions however you like, to suit the individual needs of your group (or yourself).

Opening Lines

The teacher or workshop leader gives the students or actors two or three lines of nonspecific dialog. They are to perform a scene starting with this dialog.

Some sample dialog sequences for this exercise are as follows:

1. What are you doing here?
2. I think you know.
1. Does he know you're here?
2. How stupid do you think I am? or:
1. Let me help you with that.

2. I can manage by myself.

1. We haven't got much time.

2. I know.

This exercise can be varied in a number of ways.

One possibility would be to use secret motivations for each of the characters in the scene. Refer back to Chapter 2.

The basic form of the scene may also be assigned. That is, the actors could be told to play the scene as a comedy, a tragedy, or a melodrama.

Certain aspects of the characters could be predetermined or randomly selected. Some characteristics could be assigned to force an actor to overcome specific weaknesses or habits. For example, if Actor A tends to be quiet on stage and lets his partner lead the scene, Actor A could be instructed to play a pushy, loud-mouthed character, while Actor B portrays a meek, unassuming character.

The opening dialog is just a jumping off point for the scene. It should be as vague and nonspecific as possible. The actors should be forced to immediately make choices concerning what they are talking about.

Empty Dialog

This exercise takes the Opening Dialog concept one step further. Here, all of the dialog for a short scene is given to the actors. The dialog should be about six to eight lines for each of the two characters in the scene. The dialog is intentionally vague and nonspecific. To make the scene dramatically interesting, the actors must provide their own subtext.

Subtext is what is going on between the characters but is never directly spoken. A crude example of subtext is when a play script includes stage directions on how to read a line. For example:

JANE: *(Coldly)* Of course I still love you, Steve.

The "cold" tone of voice called for in the stage direction implies that something more is going on than Jane just confirming her love for Steve. This is the subtext. In this case, the subtext (Jane's cold attitude), seems to contradict the spoken surface text ("Of course I still love you, Steve.").

In this exercise, the surface text (the actual dialog) says as little as possible. There *has* to be some subtext to give the scene some meaning. Changing the subtext totally alters the meaning of the written lines.

Here is a typical example of Empty Dialog:

1. Hello.
2. Good evening.
1. Did you bring it?
2. Of course I did.
1. Any problems?
2. Nothing I couldn't handle.
1. I wouldn't want anything to go wrong.
2. Everything will be fine.

The subtext in this particular scene hinges on just what "it" is. What did Actor 2 bring? Is it a bomb? Or is it a surprise birthday present for an unseen third character? Whatever choice the actors make about "it," it will have a very definite effect on how the scene plays, and what the lines will mean.

Here is another example of Empty Dialog:

1. Hey, you!
2. Yeah?
1. You from around here?
2. Yeah.
1. Well, you know what?
2. Yeah?
1. I don't like your face.
2. Oh, yeah?

In this case, Actor 2 faces a special challenge. Since his dialog is basically just one word repeated several times ("Yeah"), his dialog is as empty of surface text as it could be.

Each "yeah" must be said differently. The delivery of each "yeah" is based on the subtext.

Who are the characters in this scene? They apparently don't know one another, and Actor 1 seems a bit aggressive. But other than that, we really don't know anything else from the surface text or dialog.

Is Actor 1 a tough-guy gangster, and Actor 2 a frightened victim? Or maybe Actor 2 is another tough guy, itching for a fight. Or perhaps, both characters are small children in a sandbox at the park. Or maybe one character is a child and one is an adult. (And which is which?)

The possibilities are endless.

The purpose of this exercise is to strengthen the actor's imagination. In portraying almost any role beyond the most rudimentary spear carrier, the actor will need to create subtext. By definition, most subtext is not in the script. This exercise helps wean the actor away from relying too much on what is actually in the script. If you base your characterization one hundred per cent on the actual words of the script, you will almost certainly end up with a flat and rather dull characterization. I don't care how good the script is. The essence of acting cannot be reduced to the actual words of written dialog. A good actor is one who can come up with a lively and appropriate subtext. This is why some actors can steal the show in bit parts, and others are competent but forgettable in a leading role.

The actor needs to create subtext to make the part his own, and to make the character live. Without subtext, the actor is just reciting words.

Voiceless Acting

Back in Chapter 2, exercises to break the actor's reliance on dialog were presented. These exercises included Nonverbal Communication and Gibberish. In a more advanced acting workshop, you may want to take this idea even further. Have the actors perform their improvised scene in total silence. Not only are words forbidden, so are all vocalizations. The actor can't rely on direct verbal expression (dialog) or even tone of voice. He must portray his character and motivations solely through body language and facial expressions.

Can the actors communicate nonverbally well enough that they can successfully play off of one another? Does each actor know what the other's character wants? Can the audience (other students or members of the group) follow what is going on in the scene?

As a variation, you could videotape an improvised scene and then play it back with the sound turned all the way down. Does the scene make sense without the words?

Body language is an important tool for the actor. It is very difficult to communicate solely by body language, but it can be done.

Faceless Acting

This is a follow-up to the Voiceless Acting exercise described above. This exercise goes one step further, and removes facial expressions from the actor's available tools. The actors must improvise a scene while wearing concealing masks or bags over their heads. (Be sure to include eye openings so the actors can see what they are doing.)

This time, the actor can communicate only through body language.

This may sound like an impossible task, but it has been done successfully in performance situations. During the Renaissance, troupes of performers traveled from village to village putting on commedia dell'arte shows. These shows were more or less improvised from a bare-bones scenario. They featured stock characters, including Harlequin, Pantalone, the Doctor of Bologna, and Punchinello. Most of the actors performed while wearing masks, which concealed most of their faces.

Dialog was used, but as often as not, the actors spoke a different language or dialect from that used by the audience. The audiences were generally poorly educated, and were not likely to know multiple languages. Moreover, no sound rein-forcement system was available, and the performances were usually given outdoors. Those in the back of the audience prob-ably couldn't hear much, even if they understood the language used by the actors. Yet, these performances seem to have been greatly enjoyed by the audiences. The commedia dell'arte per-formers were skilled at nonverbal communication. Much of their acting was in their body language. If they could do it, there is no reason why modern actors can't learn to make the same expressive use of their bodies.

Unwritten Scenes

Of course, any improvisation is an unwritten scene. That is, the actors "write" the script as they perform it. However, I am using the term "Unwritten Scene" here in a more specific sense.

This exercise is to aid actors in developing a strong characterization while preparing for a scripted play. When directing a scripted play, I like to devote one or two rehearsals to improvisations. The actors play their characters in scenes that are not part of the play script. There are many possible scenes that could be done this way. Some suggestions follow.

Scenes that took place before the beginning of the play. Almost all plays refer directly or indirectly to earlier events. Let the actors dramatize (improvisationally) one or more past events mentioned or alluded to in the script. Another possibility is to improvise a scene in which two (or more) of the characters in the play meet.

What happens after the final curtain? With very few excep-tions, at least some characters go on with their lives after the play is over. Very few plays end with the entire cast lying dead on the floor. Improvise later scenes that might be suggested by the script.

Scenes that take place off-stage. In most plays, characters enter and exit from time to time. They don't cease to exist when they walk off-stage. If the play is set in a living room, try an improvised scene when two or more characters have exited to the bedroom or the kitchen. In some cases, the off-stage action will be implied or directly referred to in the script. When doing an "off-stage" improvisation, consider why the character exits and re-enters the scripted scene.

I suggest you read the play "Rosencrantz and Guildenstern Are Dead" by Tom Stoppard. This is not one of my favorite plays, but it illustrates what I am talking about here. Rosencrantz and Guildenstern are minor characters in "Hamlet." For most of Shakespeare's play, Rosencrantz and Guildenstern are off-stage. In Stoppard's play, we see fragments of "Hamlet" from the point of view of Rosencrantz and Guildenstern. Most of this script is comprised of off-stage action from the Shakespeare version.

Scenes with off-stage characters. Most plays refer to characters who are never seen on the stage. Sometimes these off-stage characters (and their relationships with one or more of the on-stage characters) may be important forces in the story. For example, in a play about a woman who has just left her husband, we may never see the husband on stage in the play, but he will obviously influence the action either directly or indirectly. Improvise a scene with the woman and her husband. Possibly include one or more of the other characters in the play in this improvised scene.

Of course, the off-stage character(s) is not cast. Either one of the actors in the play will need to take on an extra role in an improvisation not involving their stage character, or you will need to bring in another actor who is familiar with the play. In some cases, the director may be willing to take on an off-stage role for an improvisation rehearsal. After all, the director should know about the off-stage character as well as anybody.

Creating Scripts Through Improvisation

Improvisation can be used to create an actual script for re-performance.

For short sketches, this is just a matter of remembering pretty much what everyone did in the improvisation. The dialog may be written down in script form, or it may be kept loose. The actors know how the story goes, but the exact lines may vary from performance to performance. After a number of performances, a very polished sketch can result by keeping track of what works in the scene and what doesn't. Most of the prepared sketches performed by the Second City troupe were created in this fashion.

Improvised scenes can also be used to create full plays.

If a playwright hits a problem spot, or a place where he isn't sure where to take the plot next, an improvisational group can come in handy. The actors can portray the characters and try the scene several times, making alterations as necessary, or changing details or plot points. For instance, in a romantic scene, a playwright might consider the following possibilities (among others). The scene has Janet telling Paul she isn't really married after all.

Paul takes Janet in his arms and tells her he loves her.
Paul gets angry at Janet for lying to him.
Janet asks Paul to kiss her.
They dance first, then kiss.

Any of these possibilities might work, but no matter which choice is made, it will affect what happens next. The scene can be improvised four times to account for each of these possibilities. Which one does the playwright like best?

An improv group can create its own play as a group effort. Art is subjective, so to avoid needless and lengthy conflicts, one person should be designated the "playwright" or "editor." The group as a whole offers input, but one person ultimately has to make the final decisions.

In some cases, it might be best if the "playwright" or "editor" is not one of the actors. This will sidestep any possible ill feelings or accusations that he is giving himself the best part, or he only likes his own lines.

Keep everything democratic, but organized. A pure democracy often won't work. There are too many possibilities of opposing, but equally valid, viewpoints. One person needs to be in charge. But if creating the script is to be a group effort, the "playwright" or "editor" should not be a dictator. His job is to synthesize everyone's good input into a unified whole, which hopefully will be better than any of the individual creators could come up with on their own.

It is a very good idea to record all improvisations that might be used for later scripts. Videotape if you can, but a simple audio cassette will usually do OK.

Sometimes it is helpful to have the actors improvise a scene several times, then have everyone in the scene independently write a partial script of the scene. Each performer will remember the scene a little differently. Some will have ideas of where the scene should have gone, but didn't. Some will think of good lines that they missed while improvising. That's all OK. Each actor should write his own script the way he thinks it should be. These scripts can be in rough form. Some of the action may be summarized rather than written out. (For example, "They argue over what happened to the money until Fred comes in.")

The playwright/editor then takes all of these varying partial scripts and combines the best of each into a single, unified, and polished final script.

I have used this approach when creating original shows with high school students, and find it works well.

The playwright/editor should emphasize to the actors that their individual scripts are to be used just as a source of ideas, not a finished script. The choices in editing will be made on the basis of what works best for the show as a whole. Warn them in advance that some great lines and bits of business may have to be cut, not because of quality, but because they just don't fit into the final product. By laying down the ground rules ahead of time, you will minimize the problems of hurt feelings when favorite bits are cut out. These problems can be particularly severe with immature and/or inexperienced performers. No matter how you handle it, there will inevitably be some hurt feelings and disappointment, but if everyone understands the procedure up front, such ill feelings can usually be soothed. Be prepared to make compromises now and then.

I like using this technique. The final script is made up of the best ideas from a number of minds, instead of just one. My high school students came up with some great lines and ideas which would have never occurred to me.

Another advantage to creating a script in this fashion is that the actors will preinfluence how the characters speak. Again, in my work with high school students, I found their partial scripts helped me create believable sounding teen-aged characters who spoke like real, modern teen-agers. The slang the characters used matched those of the actual students. The characters' speech rhythms and patterns were also comfortable for the actors because they created them in the first place.

These improvisational techniques tend to work best for creating fairly simply plotted scripts. A very intricate story with lots of subplots, or a story heavy in deep psychological overtones probably wouldn't work out too well. It will be too hard to keep focus in the improvisation sessions.

Chapter Summary

There is little to say in conclusion to this chapter. Any actor who can perform these exercises well should be able to tackle almost any part on stage. You can't succeed in these advanced exercises with cheap gimmicks. You really have to be able to act.

Improvisational techniques can be very exciting, and much of that excitement can carry over into a script well crafted from improvisational work.

Probably the single most important factor in determining the success or failure of a comedy improv troupe is compatibility.

Chapter 7
FORMING A COMEDY/ IMPROV TROUPE

If you are interested in performance improvisation, the first step is, obviously, to find some other performers to work with. In other words, a troupe must be formed.

A comedy/improv troupe may be formed on a temporary basis, just for one or two shows. Generally, however, it is better to form a troupe with the idea that you are going to be together for quite some time. Performance improvisation relies very heavily on cooperation between the performers. The better they know one another, the better they will be able to improvise together.

This chapter will give you some tips on forming your own comedy/improv performance troupe.

Compatibility

Probably the single most important factor in determining the success or failure of a comedy/improv troupe is compatibility. A successful performance group is not comprised of several individual performers sharing stage time. Instead, the individual members combine to form a cohesive group identity.

The talent of the group, as a whole, is not just the sum of the talents of the members as individuals. Ideally, the members together should offer far more than they could individually.

Being a successful member of a good comedy/improv troupe is not just a question of talent alone. I have seen several groups made up of very talented individuals flop miserably. Sometimes, if the group members are too good as solo performers, they may not be able to work together cohesively as a performance troupe.

A while ago, I had an experience with a comedy/improv

troupe that illustrated the compatibility problem quite clearly. This group was formed at a local comedy club. The core of the group was made up of the club's regulars — people who had performed stand-up routines there frequently, either on Open-Mike night, or as paid opening acts. They even considered limiting admission to the group to experienced stand-up comics, although it was finally decided to include a few outsiders as "new blood."

This group had enormous compatibility problems, and only lasted a few months before disbanding. In hindsight, perhaps many of these problems are inevitable from the group's origins.

First, there was a clique problem. The group was divided into "the stand-ups" and the "nonstand-ups." This cliquishness was denied on the surface, but it had a strong, unspoken influence. For example, at rehearsals, the two subgroups sat apart from each other. The troupe's members did not feel like they were all parts of the same group. It was a case of "us and them."

Another problem was due to the past experience of the stand-up comics. They were used to working alone, holding the stage and the audience by the force of their personality. They were generally used to relying heavily on punch lines and one-liners. Good improvisation, on the other hand, absolutely demands full cooperation between the performers. It has to be a give and take situation. Moreover, punch lines and one-liners tend to be risky in performance improv. If you rely too heavily on formula jokes, the performance will only be as good as the last punch line. If several one-liners fall flat, the audience will be lost. Even if they don't physically leave, emotionally they will have left the performers. It will be very difficult to win them back.

There was also a tendency on the part of the stand-up comics to throw in bits of their stand-up act whenever an appropriate cue was given. For example, if dating was mentioned, out would come the stock gags about dates. This was a natural enough tendency. Improvisation is inherently risky, especially if you are strongly joke oriented, so it is only natural to use any tried and true material. Unfortunately, this leads to a certain amount of repetition and a loss of the improvisational sparkle. The performances often didn't feel spontaneous, because they weren't.

Some of the stand-up comics did better than others. (At least one was a real delight to work with.) But their past experience set an unexpected barrier for them. They had to fight to overcome habits that were appropriate to a stand-up performance, but unsuited to improvisation.

Clearly, it would be a grave mistake to try to form a comedy/improv troupe with membership restricted to stand-up comics. That is not to say that stand-up comics should be barred from joining a comedy/improv troupe. Don't shut out talent wherever you find it. But if the group is entirely made up of stand-up comics, it will be next to impossible for them to overcome their stand-up habits. It may even be difficult for them to determine just what the problem is.

Of course, a group of stand-up comics may decide to get together and perform a little improv in a show, if they are so inclined. But if they are planning on building a continuing performance troupe, they should try to get some members with differing backgrounds.

Compatibility in a comedy/improv troupe is partially a matter of give and take. The performers must work together and help each other on-stage. The performers should not compete with one another.

Another factor in group compatibility is personality. The troupe members must get along with one another, or they certainly won't be able to work well together. This is not to say you must be best friends off-stage. You don't have to socialize together if you don't want to, but you need to respect one another as individuals, and more importantly, you must respect each other as performers. There should not be a star and supporting players. While one performer may be the center of one scene, all are equally important to the troupe.

For some performers, it may be helpful if they are not off-stage friends. Too strong a personal attachment might get in the way of reacting to each other as different characters with different relationships.

Another problem with the comedy club troupe I was talking about earlier was severe personality conflicts. This broke up the cohesiveness of the troupe, and got in the way of a group identity.

Still another aspect of group compatibility is style compatibility. Two performers may be highly talented, and they may respect each other enormously, but they still may be a disaster when they get on stage together. Their performance styles must fit together. Some performers lean towards realism and quiet irony, while others may go in for wild farce and melodramatic overplaying. One or both performers must be able to compromise their style to work together well. Otherwise, they will seem to be playing entirely different scenes, even though they're both on-stage at the same time.

Performance styles may also be problematic if they are too similar. To play off of one another, there must be some contrast between the players. There is one fellow I have worked with on several occasions. When we improvise together, the results are often rather flat because we both tend to work in a dry, deadpan style. To improvise well together, one (or both) of us must make a conscious effort to alter our performance style to give the other something to play off of. Incidentally, even though we don't improvise well together, the similarity of our styles makes us good writing partners. Let me emphasize, compatibility of problems in a comedy/improv troupe is not a question of individual talent.

One final factor in group compatibility is one which is difficult to define or concretely identify, even though it is unmistakable when it is there. This element could be called, for want of a better term, "chemistry."

When a group has good chemistry, the whole is far greater than the sum of the parts. This is, the performers seem better together than they do separately, or teamed with someone else.

There is that extra sparkle and magic. If talent could be quantified, A could have fifty per cent talent, and B have fifty per cent talent, but the combination of A plus B would have one hundred fifty per cent talent. The extra fifty per cent comes from the chemistry between the performers — that something special that happens when they get together.

Chemistry between performers is one of those things that is impossible to predict. It often turns up in some very unexpected combinations. And when it shows up, it's wonderful.

Sometimes a couple of performers may have bad chemistry with one another. They may be great friends off-stage, but on-stage, the combination just doesn't work. If this is the case, the two performers should avoid working together. Fortunately, true bad performance chemistry is rarer than good performance chemistry. For most combinations of performers, the effects of chemistry will be negligible. This factor can generally be ignored unless it is strong enough that it just can't be ignored. In that case, by all means, go for it.

Leadership

If you are forming a new comedy/improv troupe, the leader of the group is an important issue you will have to consider.

Without some kind of leader, the troupe will flounder. In a group of creative people, such as improvisation performers, disagreements will unquestionably arise. The leader and organization of the troupe should help resolve such difficulties before they become critical problems.

Many comedy/improv troupes have a definite leader. This will usually be the group's founder, and the person with the most relevant experience. The leader is responsible for all decisions concerning the group. What will be rehearsed when? What structures will be included in a given performance and in what order? Which performers will appear in each structure?

The leader's most important function is to act as a focal point for the troupe. A conglomeration of creative people, such as a comedy/improv troupe, will often try to fly off in several directions at once. One direction isn't necessarily better than another, but the group can only successfully go in one direction at a time. A cohesive group identity is important to the success of your troupe. The audience (and more importantly, the prospective audience) should recognize your group name and know more or less what can be expected from your performances. The leader directs the focus of the group, and makes decisions as to style.

Of course, a good leader, especially in this type of group, should not play dictator. All members of the group should be permitted to offer input and suggestions. In some cases, a vote may be taken. But overall, someone needs to make the final decisions. This is the role of the leader. With one person definitely in charge, there will be a certain consistency of style in all decisions. I'm not talking about falling into a predictable rut. I'm talking about a consistent image so that audiences can recognize your group as a group. It's a matter of organization.

The leader should not be "the star" with everyone else as his "supporting players." Everyone is of equal importance to the group.

In some of the improv troupes I've led, my name has been billed along with the group's name. I usually served as emcee and host for the performances. In this sense I was the "star" of the show. I was the most noticeable individual. I used my name in publicity because I also worked as a solo performer and had some reputation and following. The cross advertising helped both my solo and group performances. I emcee simply because I enjoy it, and I seem to be pretty good at it. Many other performers seem uncomfortable being emcee. So there were good reasons for my pseudo-star status. But I fought to keep it from going past this nominal level. I tried to give the other members of the troupe ample stage time and credit. I often took supporting and minor roles in prepared sketches. I did not structure the performances to support my "star" status.

By taking this approach, and discussing the matter with the group, I believe I was able to avoid the ill feelings and jealousies a "star" can generate. It is a tricky issue. It often comes up for me because there are relatively few experienced improv performers. When I start a new troupe, most of the members are totally inexperienced, so I am automatically placed in a teacher/mentor role. Less experienced performers often prefer the security of an experienced nominal "star" who can bail them out of performance problems, if necessary.

I always tell my troupe members I want them to be better than I am. "I want you all to be so good, I'll feel guilty casting myself. I want you to be strong enough at performing, that the only thing I need to do is introduce you." And I mean that. I'm lazy. Let them do the work. Actually, I am less a performer, and am more interested in directing, so I really would be content with emceeing the show.

Some groups may prefer to work with a more fully democratic system. Everyone gets an equal vote in all important decisions. This is admirable and can work, but you still need someone to make the smaller day-to-day decisions, and to organize and schedule rehearsals, performances, publicity, and the like. If you are uncomfortable with the idea of a leader or president, elect a coordinator instead. This title best describes the leadership function in a democratic group anyway.

The coordinator casts tie-breaking votes, organizes rehearsals, determines the running order of shows, and makes the other decisions that have to be made but don't really require extensive input or debate from the group at large. Without a strong coordinator, it is all too easy for the group to bog down into lengthy discussions (and sometimes heated arguments) over whether structure A should come before or after structure B.

Rehearsal time can also be wasted without a good coordinator to organize it. Without a coordinator, the group members will drift in and waste a half hour or even more trying to decide which structures to rehearse and in what order. The coordinator should arrive at the rehearsal with a schedule. For example, "Today we are going to work on Story, Story, and Double Emotions. Let's get to work." Of course, the coordinator's schedule should not be inflexible. Group members should be allowed to have input. For example, one member might suggest, "I think we need more work on Freeze Tag." The coordinator should then find time to rehearse that structure, either during the current rehearsal, or the next one.

The group's coordinator also serves as a focal point for the group, although to a lesser degree than a full leader.

In a democratic group, the coordinator should be elected, although, if one person has served as the founder and has done the work of getting the troupe together in the first place, it's not unreasonable for him to serve as the coordinator for the first term.

The elected coordinator should have a definite term of office. It should not be permanent, nor should it be indefinite. Some groups may elect a coordinator with the option of voting him out of office at a later date. This will almost inevitably lead to hard feelings and ill will. It's better to have a definite term of office, after which the former coordinator may or may not be re-elected.

Do not make the term of office for the coordinator too long. I'd say one year is about the maximum. On the other hand, if the term is too short, you'll end up with chaos and massive disorganization. The minimum term of office, in my opinion, should be about three to six months.

Group Composition

When forming a new comedy/improv troupe, you also need to give some consideration to the composition of the group. How many performing members should there be? Should there be a limit to the age range? Should all of the performers be about the same age, or will you work with a wide range of ages? How young is too young, and how old is too old?

Do you want to include any specific physical types? How much experience should the performers have, and how much?

These questions must be considered at the onset, or you may well run into serious problems in forming your comedy/improv troupe.

Setting Goals

What are the goals of your comedy/improv troupe? Is it to be a continuing group, or will you be together for just a short time? Is the purpose of the group primarily educational (for the performers)? Or are you interested in putting on the most professional shows possible? Are the group's future goals professional or amateur?

These factors should be decided upon right at the start. Of course, you could conceivably change your mind on one or all of these issues at a later date. That's OK. But you need to know what direction you're trying to go in, or you aren't going to go anywhere.

By having a firm grasp of your specific goals you will have an easier time determining who will fit into the troupe, and who will not. Knowing your goals will give you a basis for deciding whether or not to accept questionable gigs, such as unpaid performances, or out-of-town jobs.

Will you be using any props, scenery, or costumes? Should there be a coordinated look to your group? Should the performers dress alike or similarly on stage? Do you want to have troupe jackets or sweat shirts made up? Should your group own its own stage equipment (microphones, amplifiers, lights, etc.)?

Record your performances and rehearsals as much as possible. Reviewing these tapes later is the best possible way to learn what works and what doesn't for you. What parts of your performance do you enjoy watching, and what parts make you cringe?

Videotape is the best choice because you can both see and hear the performance. If this is not practical, you can still get some value out of recording performances and rehearsals on audio cassette.

Naming Your Group

Any comedy/improv troupe needs a name. After all, how can there be a group identity if the group is unidentified?

Think carefully about the name you choose. It should express what your group is all about and give some indication of your style. It should be catchy and memorable.

Your group's name is your most basic and direct (and sometimes only) form of advertising. For most of your audience, the name will be all they know about you when they walk into one of your performances. Choose a name that will pique your audience's interest.

Avoid triteness in your group's name. A trite group name subtly suggests a lack of originality, which is deadly for an improv troupe. Avoid using obvious words in your group name. If a word seems like an obvious choice, it is almost certainly trite. Poor word choices include: crazy, funny, lunatic, nuts, wacky, zany.

On the other hand, try to avoid going too far out. To use an example from television, one of the original name choices for the group that became "Monty Python's Flying Circus" was "Owl Stretching Time." This is certainly clever and very original, but it is likely to put some of the potential audience off right at the start. There is a fine line between cleverly outrageous and too outrageous.

For one improv troupe I created, we decided we liked the word "spontaneous." That is certainly an appropriate word for an improv troupe, but is off-beat enough to avoid triteness. Now, "Spontaneous —" what?

One suggestion came out — "Spontaneous Human Combustion." Yes, that was a funny idea, but probably not a very good name. Many people are likely to say, "I don't want to see anything called 'Spontaneous Human Combustion.'" And I can't really blame them. The name is just a little too outrageous.

After applying a little more brainwork, we came up with a name I still think works beautifully. "Spontaneous Intentions." It is an outrageous oxymoron, but it sounds like fun. And it seemed pretty catchy. Talking with some audience members after the first couple of shows, I learned that many were drawn in by the name. They had to find out what it was all about.

For another group, we decided to emphasize that we were struggling unknowns striving for recognition, so we called the group "No One in Particular." This title also seemed to draw positive attention.

If you are unsure of a potential name, try it out on a number of people uninvolved with your group. Asking friends for their opinion is fine, but you'll get a better feel of how the name really works by asking strangers. Just hang around a busy corner or a shopping mall and survey passers-by. Some people will refuse to respond (sometimes rather rudely), but most people will be happy to answer one or two short questions. "Excuse me, Ma'am. We're forming a comedy/improv troupe, and we'd like to know what you think of the name —. Thank you." Most people will be flattered to be asked for their opinion, if you don't take up too much of their time.

A strong name probably isn't going to help a mediocre improv troupe. If you don't put on a good show, the audience isn't going to come back for your next performance, no matter what you call yourselves. But it is entirely possible that a good group may be hurt by a poor name.

Finding an opportunity to perform may require calling local nightclubs, bars, coffee houses and theatres. Most won't be interested.

Chapter 8
PUTTING ON AN IMPROV SHOW

While improvisation should be, by definition, spontaneous, to do it well generally requires extensive rehearsal. The rules of the structures must become second nature. The performer should not have to think about the rules. He should be able to concentrate entirely on his role within the improvisation.

Rehearsal is also vital for the various performers to work well together. You have to know your partner's stage technique and how his mind works. Good improvisation is true give and take. That can only come after extensive rehearsal.

Finding a Place to Perform

Once your comedy/improv troupe is well rehearsed, you will need to find a suitable outlet for your group's skills and talents. Rehearsing together is fun, but if you are a performance group, your ultimate goal, obviously, is to perform before an audience.

What performance opportunities are available in your area? Check into local nightclubs, bars, coffee houses and theatres. Some will not be interested in offering any entertainment. Some will only be interested in their present in-house talent and will not welcome outsiders. But many managers are interested in offering entertainment to their customers if they can find the right talent for the right price. In some cases, it might be worthwhile to do a performance or two without pay, just to prove yourselves. Whet the audience's appetite for more of your performances, and the management will usually be willing to pay you for more.

Adjust your performances to suit the type of performance space. Nightclubs and bars will generally call for very different performance styles than coffee houses or theatres. In a night-club or bar, the audience is drinking, or perhaps eating. They may be placing orders during your performance. You will have to work that much harder to grab and hold their attention. Humor for a drinking audience will often be broader and less intellectual. If you are inclined towards "blue" material, a nightclub/bar environment may work well with you.

Very sophisticated material or any bit which doesn't reach its point quickly will probably fail before a drinking crowd. If the audience is drinking, they can't be expected to participate with the improvisations on a high level. It would be best to avoid the advanced structures described in Chapter 5 if you're working before a drinking audience. Either the piece will fall flat, or some members of the audience may misunderstand their role and over-participate or participate inappropriately, resulting in total chaos.

Remember, in a bar or nightclub, much of the audience is there primarily for the drinks, and the performance is secondary. They may regard it as a fringe benefit, or they may be annoyed by it.

On the other hand, in a coffee house, or especially a theatre, the performance is more important to the audience. They came to see a show.

Theatre and coffee house audiences are generally reasonably bright and well-educated. They will tend to appreciate wit. Some broad humor is OK, but a little bit goes a long way. The audience will tend to get bored and restless if they aren't challenged at all.

Obviously, different performing troupes will be more comfortable and work better in different performing environments. Some groups are able to perform well both in nightclubs/bars and in coffee houses/theatres. Other groups would be well advised to stick with one category or the other.

Another possibility is to rent your own performance space. Most towns and cities have various places available for rent, although finding them usually requires some legwork.

Call any organization which might possibly have a space available for rent. Try any possibility you can come up with. Sometimes the best prospects are found in the most unlikely places.

Expect to be turned down by most of the organizations you approach. Just because they have a space that can be used for performance doesn't necessarily mean they are willing to rent it out to other groups, especially unknown groups.

Other organizations welcome the extra income from renting out their space when they are not using it themselves. You will almost certainly have to adapt your schedule to suit the organization that owns the space.

Some typical possibilities for renting performance space include schools, meeting halls and churches.

In some cases, the host organization may want to have a say in the material presented. This will usually be the case for most churches and many schools. Your group will have to decide whether or not they can live with the renting organization's restrictions. Some groups will just want reassurance that you are not going to be offensive. Since you are performing in their space, the public will tend to associate what you do with the renting organization. A church, for example, probably wouldn't appreciate scatalogical, obscene or sacrilegious humor. Such restrictions are fair and reasonable. If the renting organization insists on a restriction you don't want to be stuck with, find another performance space.

Other organizations may be very heavy on full censorship. They'll want to know everything you're going to do ahead of time. They may want script approval. Obviously, this won't work out well for an improv troupe. Find another place to perform. Because you are performing improvisations, there is no way all of your material can be approved beforehand. Major conflicts are almost certain. This is a bad situation which should be avoided at all costs.

A few organizations won't care about the content of your performance at all, as long as it is not illegal or in any way harmful to the space. Naturally, no organization is likely to be happy about you damaging any of their property.

Before signing any contract to rent a performance space, be sure to be absolutely clear on the rules of the organization. Don't be surprised after the fact. What, if any, control do they want over your performances? What responsibilities will be expected of you? (Most organizations that rent space will require that you clean up the space after each use.) What dates will the space be available? When will it definitely be unavailable? Of course, it is vital to agree upon the rent itself before signing anything.

Programming

Much of the success of your show will be determined by how it is programmed. What pieces (or structures) will be performed and in what order?

Your opening piece should be strong to catch the audience's interest. Convince it right at the start that they're in for a good show. A proven prescripted piece is often the best choice for the opening. An improvisation can be risky. By definition, sometimes improvs work, and sometimes they don't.

If you do open the show with an improv, select a strong, but relatively simple structure which calls for a bare minimum of input from the audience. You can't assume it will really know what's going on and be into the spirit of improvisation right at the start of the show. Ease the audience into it.

Unless your show is very, very short, it is strongly advised that you include some prepared pieces in among the improvs. If you do nothing but improvisation, the show will almost undoubtedly suffer from "improv burn-out." Improvs are a very intense form of performance. They take a lot out of both the performers and the audience. Everybody can get exhausted if you don't ease up on the intensity once in awhile. Throw in some prepared pieces (perhaps refined from earlier improv performances) to vary the pace of the show from time to time. Remember, too much of a good thing can be exhausting and lead to rapidly declining quality.

The ratio of scripted (prepared) scenes to improvs will

depend to a large extent on the make-up and interests of your group. As a rule of thumb, for any performance of an hour or more, more than fifty per cent improvisation is probably too much.

If your group is only interested in performing improvisationally and you don't really want to do any prepared pieces, then team up with some other act, such as a band. Do a show together, alternately. The band plays a couple of songs, then the improv troupe does a couple of scenes, followed by a few more songs by the band, and then more improvs. Just don't overload the audience with too much improvisation all at once.

It is also important to watch out for too many similar improv structures, especially back to back. If you seem to be doing pretty much the same thing over and over, the audience will start to grow bored and unimpressed with your improvisational abilities, no matter how clever you are. Variety is the key here.

Selecting the Emcee

Who will emcee your show? Except in very unusual circumstances, the emcee should be a member of your troupe.

The emcee is the audience's point of connection to the show and to the troupe as a whole. The emcee should be efficient, but warm. He doesn't have to gush, but he's got to give the appearance that he is welcoming the audience into the fun.

The emcee must also be able to clearly and succinctly explain each improv structure to the audience. He must let them know what to expect and what is expected of them. That is, the audience must understand what kind of suggestions it must make.

If the emcee has an easy humor, great. The emcee can be funny, but not overpowering. It is *not* the emcee's show. The emcee's function is to serve as a guide. He keeps the show on track. The emcee is not the star.

Generally, a single emcee should be used throughout the

entire show. His presence helps hold the show together. He is the audience's link to the show. Of course, the emcee may also perform in some of the improv structures or prepared pieces too.

Some groups take turns being emcee in each new show. This is a useful approach if the majority all want to do the job, or, just as common, if nobody really wants the task. The emcee is out in the spotlight, but it really isn't a very glamorous role. Some people enjoy it, and some don't.

In other groups, one person will more or less be the permanent emcee for the troupe. This is the obvious choice when you have one strong, willing emcee-type performer, without any competition for the job.

Some improv troupes like to use different emcees for each structure. This is risky. It breaks up the continuity of the show.

There is a simple compromise that can clear up the difficulty here. You have one main emcee for the show as a whole. But anybody in the troupe may serve as a structure emcee (the emcee role outlined in the descriptions of the improv structures in Chapters 3 through 5). The main emcee introduces the structure and then turns the stage over to the structure emcee.

Dealing With Audience Problems

In an improv show, the audience is part of the performance. Inevitably some people in certain audiences will present a problem of one sort or another. There are countless potential problems (most, fortunately, are relatively rare), so there is no way I can tell you how to deal with all possibilities. But I will try to offer a few tips on dealing with common audience problems.

If you are starting a new group in an area where there hasn't been much improvisational performance, the audience may be reluctant to participate at first. They are either afraid of interfering with a preset piece, or they are afraid of making an inappropriate response and looking foolish. This is one reason why the emcee should seem warm and friendly. Part of his job is to loosen up the audience.

If you have problems with an unresponsive audience, first make sure that they understand what is expected of them. Offer a few examples of the kind of responses you are looking for. For instance, "Name an emotion, like love or fear, or something like that."

If no one responds, the emcee can ask specific individuals in the audience for suggestions. "You, sir, name a place, any place at all."

Some groups may have plants (confederates) in the audience. If no one responds, the plant can start the ball rolling with a suggestion or two. Whenever possible, the plant should just get the audience started. It's not good improv to take a prearranged suggestion from an audience plant. But if the audience won't cooperate, a planted suggestion can at least allow you to keep the show moving.

Sometimes you will have the opposite problem. The audience (or certain people in the audience) will keep shouting out things, even when you don't need or want audience suggestions. This can be a problem after a structure that calls for a lot of audience participation, like Fill in the Blank, especially if the audience has been drinking.

The emcee should say in a firm, but friendly manner something like, "OK, that's all we need from you now. Your job is done."

Almost any performer or performing group sooner or later has to deal with hecklers. Hecklers are particularly common in drinking audiences, but they can show up anywhere. If you are doing comedy, hecklers often think they are helping you out. They really aren't, but you can't convince them of that.

If possible, ignore mild heckling. Don't draw attention to it, or you might get more.

If you must react to it, be firm, but polite. Stock put-downs like those used by some stand-up comics tend to encourage hecklers rather than discourage them. A heckler wants attention. By throwing a funny squelch line at him, you are putting him in the spotlight. It will rarely shut him up.

To avoid audience problems, the emcee's instructions to the audience should be as clear and specific as possible. Often, audience members may misunderstand, and create problems. Once again, such problems are most frequent when the audience has been drinking, but they can show up in any performance environment.

I'll give you one example from my own personal experience. I was in an improv troupe that was working in a comedy club/bar. The emcee introduced Freeze Tag by saying, "Anyone can jump in by yelling 'freeze' and taking the place of one of the performers in the scene." One guy in the audience assumed "anyone" included him, and not just anyone in the troupe. He kept shouting "Freeze!" and trying to crawl up on stage. Fortunately, he was with some friends who managed to hold him back. From then on, our emcee was always careful to specify that "any of the performers can yell 'freeze'."

The emcee's introductions should be carefully thought out in advance to avoid any problematic ambiguities like that.

Never sign a contract that gives someone else exclusive rights to your name or likeness.

Chapter 9
PROTECTING YOURSELF AND YOUR WORK

Everyone who improvises is, by definition, a writer, whether they put anything down on paper or not. In improvisation the performers are writing their own script as they go along.

You have legal and moral rights with regard to the creations of your mind.

Unfortunately for many artistic types, business dealings are an inevitable part of establishing and running a comedy/improv troupe.

Many beginners are so eager for any chance to perform that they will accept unquestionably bad deals and foolishly sign away future rights (and possible profits) to their work just for the chance of exposure today.

Negotiating Contracts and Deals

If an outside individual or organization (such as a nightclub) is sponsoring your comedy/improv troupe, it probably is not doing so out of the kindness of its heart. It wants to turn a profit from its sponsorship. There is nothing wrong with this, as long as it is a fair profit. Newcomers going up against an established business can be badly cheated if they don't work to preserve their own rights.

In any negotiation, a smart businessman will ask for everything. He will even ask for things he doesn't particularly want because these things can be used as bargaining points for the things he really does want. In business, it only makes sense to get the best deal for yourself you can. Ask for the moon, even if there doesn't seem to be much chance that you'll get it.

Most businessmen expect their first offer to be rejected,

opening up negotiation. Negotiation, like improvisation, is a give and take process. "I'll accept points A and B, if you'll delete point C and replace it with point D." The goal is to reach a compromise that is fair and acceptable to both parties.

If your first offer is the bare minimum you'll accept, there isn't much chance that the other guy will offer you a better deal. And if the other party rejects your bare minimum offer, the deal is off. You've left yourself no room to negotiate and compromise. Go ahead, ask for more than you want or need. It's not greedy or dishonest. It's just the way business deals work. If you are dealing with an established business, it's not likely that they'll let you cheat them. They won't accept a deal that is unfair to them, and neither should you.

If a potential sponsor for your group makes a demand you don't like, negotiate. If you can't live with the terms of the demand, do not accept any deal involving that demand.

Even if the demand is only mildly negative, but you could live with it, try to negotiate it out of the deal anyway. You never know, it may not be an important point to the other guy. He might be willing to drop the demand. Or he might be willing to trade his demand for one of yours.

Dangerous Contract Clauses

There are a few demands that may show up in offered contracts that you should avoid at all possible costs. It is in the sponsor's interest to ask for these things, but they are very unfair to you (the creator/performer). Insist that they be removed from the contract. Most honest sponsors will agree to negotiate these points. If they are dead set on these unfair clauses, they probably aren't someone you should be doing business with anyway.

Even if it means killing the deal, don't accept any blatantly unfair conditions.

Watch out for the word "exclusive." It usually means trouble.

Never, ever sign any contract which gives someone

else exclusive rights to your name or likeness, especially for a long or unspecified term or forever. During the term of the contract, you cannot work for anyone else or perform in public without the permission of the person or firm holding the contract. To do any outside work at all, you'd have to use an assumed name and disguise your appearance.

The exclusive rights to name and likeness clause is a standardized item in many contracts, even though the contract writer assumes that it will be used as a point of negotiation and will eventually be deleted. But every once in a while, a naive writer or performer will sign a contract with this clause still in it. They will inevitably regret it sooner or later. Personally, I believe there should be a law against including such a clause in any contract, as it is always extremely unfair.

Some contracts will ask for exclusive performances for the contract owner. That means, for the duration of the contract, you cannot work for anyone else (in the same field, of course) without the contract owner's prior approval. Try to get rid of the word "exclusive" in such a clause. This won't always be possible. Nobody wants to hire you and have you simultaneously work for their competition. For example, let's say there are two comedy clubs in a given town. One is called "Laugh Trax" and the other is "Ho-Ho's." (These are made-up names. I am not aware of any businesses using these names, but coincidences are possible.) As a beginner, you sign a contract with Laugh Trax. They groom you and allow you to polish your act. As you build a reputation, you will start drawing customers to the club. If you also work for Ho-Ho's, many people will be coming to see you there instead of at Laugh Trax. Laugh Trax will see the profit going to their competitor.

Exclusive performance clauses can be reasonable. On the other hand, it is in the performer's interest to avoid them, as they, by definition, limit the work he may do. Negotiate to reach the best deal for both parties.

An exclusive performance clause should be for a specific time period only. The length of the restriction should not be indefinite. Ideally, from the performer's point of view, the restriction term should be as short as possible.

A cancellation clause of some sort should also be included. If the contract owner is not providing you with a sufficient amount of work (the amount should be specified in the contract), he should allow you to find outside sources of income.

There is a world of difference between a fair and legitimate business contract and indentured servitude.

The important thing is to know what you are signing and what the consequences might be ahead of time. Have a lawyer read through any contract and explain all of the clauses to you before signing anything.

Characters and Material

Some contracts will grant the contract holder exclusive rights to the material you create while working for them. Again, avoid the exclusive clause, if you can. It is in your interest to be able to reuse your own material at a later date.

Sometimes the contract holder will just own a piece of the material. That is, any time in the future that you are paid for performing the material, you must pay a percentage to the original contract holder.

Avoid such clauses if you can, but sometimes you will have to give in to such demands. Try to retain as much ownership of your own material as you can.

Even if the contract owner retains rights to material created while you're working for him, try not to give him rights to any of your characterizations. Many a performer's career has been made successful by a character that really works. You obviously want to own such a character free and clear. Don't even consider signing away future rights to any character you might create. Somebody else might become a star playing a character you created.

Copyrights

It is a good idea to get a copyright on any script you write. Under current copyright laws, the copyright is automatic. As soon as you write it, it is legally yours, unless you sell the rights. A written script should have a copyright notice at the bottom of the first page or the title page. Acceptable forms are as follows: "Copyright 1990 by Delton T. Horn," or, "© 1990, Delton T. Horn."

This notice must be on any copy that is published, or distributed to the public. If a work is published without the legal notice, you may lose your copyright. On the other hand, private copies not intended for the general public don't necessarily require a specific copyright notice. It is assumed.

You can also file for copyright protection with the Copyright Office in Washington, D.C. Write to this address: Information and Publishing Section, LM-455, Copyright Office, Library of Congress, Washington, D.C. 20559, or call (202) 287-8700.

For scripts, ask for Form PA.

There is a fee for each filing with the Copyright Office. Currently this fee is ten dollars. You don't need to file each sketch separately. Combine several sketches into a collection or revue and file them as a single script.

You will need to file with the Copyright Office before starting any legal action for copyright infringement. Other than that, filing isn't really essential under the current copyright laws.

It can be worthwhile to mail yourself a copy of the script. Do not open the envelope. The postmark on the sealed envelope can be offered as proof that the material was in your possession as of the date of the postmark. This doesn't absolutely prove copyright ownership, but it may demonstrate that you had the material at an earlier time than someone else.

For an improv group, official copyright filing is inappropriate because there is no written script to file, unless you transcribe it after the fact. Automatic copyright protection is still yours under the law. If you are broadcasting on the radio or television, include a copyright notice in the credits. For example,

"Contents of this program copyright 1986, by 'No One in Particular' and Delton T. Horn." This spoken notice isn't essential, but it can help in certain conflicts.

A statement of copyright is not needed for a performance before a live audience.

Existing Characters

Sometimes in an improv performance, you will want to use a known character, either real or fictional. Usually this is perfectly all right under "Fair Use" laws. You can do an improv or even a sketch involving George Bush or John Wayne. As public figures, they are open to reasonable use. They are part of the public consciousness. As long as you are not attempting to impersonate the public figure for fraudulent or illegal purposes, or for purposes of libel, you are OK. In a comic or improv sketch, libel usually isn't a problem since you are obviously and openly dealing with fictional material. In almost all cases, you will be working with the public perception of the public figures rather than revealing any private information about them. This is within the legal definition of Fair Use.

Generally speaking, you can do short and improvised material involving fictional characters owned by someone else, such as Donald Duck or E.T., without permission, *if* it is clear that you are not "stealing" legitimate use of the character. For example, an improvised scene about Donald Duck applying for a bank loan isn't likely to infringe on the rights of the Disney Studios.

However, permission from the owners will probably be required if you make extensive or repeated use of an owned character. If Donald Duck is always a part of your show, you better get permission, especially if you advertise or publicize the use of the characterization. If you don't get prior permission, there is a good chance you will be hearing from Disney's lawyers. They own the character. They don't want someone else to profit from their creation. Of course, a character like Donald Duck or Superman has entered into the public consciousness as a standardized symbol. It is reasonable to claim

Fair Use of a public symbol.

For example, I have often used a sketch I wrote (which started out as an improvisation) about a group therapy session for super heroes. Owned characters such as Wonder Woman, The Flash, and Captain America appear in this piece. They refer to Superman a lot, even though he does not appear on stage.

The satirical intent of this piece is unmistakable. Obviously, I am using the characters outside their normal, intended context. I am in no way in competition with the copyright and trademark holders for these characters. I am using public images for comic purposes, which is within the restraints defined by Fair Use laws.

Fair Use is a tricky concept. When in doubt, get permission from the lawful owners of the character, or seek legal advice.

Of course, in an improv troupe, prior arrangements often can't be made. Audiences will frequently suggest well-known fictional and real-life characters and settings. For example, one of my favorite improvisation set-ups was about Mrs. Santa Claus and her lover, G. Gordon Liddy, aboard the starship Enterprise. (We had the suggestion of Mrs. Santa Claus, then we heard two suggestions for the other character simultaneously — her lover and G. Gordon Liddy. So we put them both together.)

Obviously, there is no problem with Mrs. Santa Claus. She is a mythical figure in the public domain. Mrs. Santa Claus is not owned by anybody. She belongs to the general public. Anyone may freely use the character.

G. Gordon Liddy is a real person. But his status as a public figure makes this use of his name Fair Use. No one would ever assume we were really claiming that G. Gordon Liddy was, in reality, the lover of Mrs. Santa Claus.

The starship Enterprise is owned by the Star Trek people, but this too is clearly Fair Use. We were obviously not trying to create a bogus "Star Trek." We were using a publicly recognizable symbol, so it's Fair Use.

In improvisation, you are generally well within Fair Use on audience suggestions since anything the audience suggests must, obviously, be part of the public consciousness.

Chapter Summary

Of course, a book like this cannot possibly offer individual legal advice, especially in a brief chapter like this. If you have any questions or have any specific problems, contact a qualified attorney, preferably one with experience in the field of entertainment and performance law.

ABOUT THE AUTHOR

Delton T. Horn is a professional freelance writer, with over 40 nonfiction books published. He is also a playwright, director, actor, and comedian. He has appeared in over 70 amateur plays, and has worked semi-professionally as a stand-up comedian.

Mr. Horn's performance specialty is sketch comedy. He has participated in several comedy troupes, often using improvisational material. Two groups, which he founded and led were "No One In Particular," and "Spontaneous Intentions." In 1986 he had his own weekly half-hour comedy show on radio in Columbia, Missouri, for six months. This program, which was aired live, was called "Without A Net." This was followed by thirty episodes of a five minute comedy serial called "Narrowed Horizons."

Among his current projects, he is working on a one-man show consisting of comic and dramatic monologs about romantic relationships.

Delton T. Horn also composes music as a hobby. Other interests include science, metaphysics, comparative religions, and old films. He steadfastly refuses to reveal what the "T" stands for.